Designing Instruction
for Library Users

Additional Volumes in Preparation

Designing Instruction for Library Users

A Practical Guide

Marilla D. Svinicki
Center for Teaching Effectiveness
The University of Texas at Austin
Austin, Texas

Barbara A. Schwartz
Barbara A. Schwartz & Associates
Austin, Texas

CRC Press
Taylor & Francis Group
Boca Raton London New York

CRC Press is an imprint of the
Taylor & Francis Group, an **informa** business

First published 1988 by Marcel Dekker, Inc.

Published 2019 by CRC Press
Taylor & Francis Group
6000 Broken Sound Parkway NW, Suite 300
Boca Raton, FL 33487-2742

© 1988 by Taylor & Francis Group, LLC
CRC Press is an imprint of Taylor & Francis Group, an Informa business

First issued in paperback 2019

No claim to original U.S. Government works

ISBN 13: 978-0-367-45138-7 (pbk)
ISBN 13: 978-0-8247-7820-0 (hbk)

Visit the Taylor & Francis Web site at
http://www.taylorandfrancis.com

and the CRC Press Web site at
http://www.crcpress.com

Library of Congress Cataloging-in-Publication Data

Svinicki, Marilla D. , [date]
    Designing instruction for library users: a practical guide /
Marilla D. Svinicki, Barbara A. Schwartz.
        p. cm. – (Books in library and information science ; vol. 50)
    Includes index.
    ISBN 0-8247-7820-0
    1. College students–Library orientation. 2. Library orientation.
3. Libraries and readers. 4. Bibliography–Methodology–Study
and teaching. I. Schwartz, Barbara A. II. Title. III. Series:
Books in library and information science ; v. 50.
Z675.U5S835 1988
025.5'677–dc19   87-22502
                                                        CIP

To Jay and Neal

Preface

This book was written for the academic librarian who has responsibility for teaching students library skills. The material presented here is the product of many years of experience working both with university students, on the front lines as a user education librarian, and with other librarians, as workshop leaders and conference speakers.

Our collaboration began in 1979, when we designed and taught a workshop series on teaching effectiveness for the professional staff of the General Libraries, The University of Texas at Austin. From there we worked together and separately on similar workshops and presentations, reaching librarians who shared the goal of improving their teaching skills.

In all of these endeavors, we emphasized the fact that there is no single "right" approach to teaching library skills; everything depends on the content or objectives of the instruction, the sophistication and motivation levels of the learners, the amount of time and type of facilities available for teaching, and the instructor's own strengths and weaknesses. Good teaching, therefore, requires careful planning; the instructor must thoughtfully analyze each of the factors affecting the instructional situation and then choose a teaching method and evaluation system accordingly. This process, called instructional design, is the focus of this book.

In the chapters that follow, we discuss the principles of learning theory and instructional design, and their application to library instruction. Our emphasis throughout the text is the application of theory to real-life situations. In addition to practical advice, however, we intend to provide the reader with the theoretical framework needed for design decision-making.

We wish to thank the librarians and faculty of The University of Texas at Austin who provided or critiqued the library assignments that form the basis of the case studies in Chapter 6.

Marilla D. Svinicki
Barbara A. Schwartz

Contents

1
Overview and Definitions

Have you ever looked closely at a painting by an old master like Da Vinci? Something like the Mona Lisa? From a distance, it balances so beautifully and looks as if it required little effort because it seems so natural. On closer inspection, however, the work reveals the careful combination of brush strokes and medium with a knowledge of anatomy and physics, plus a touch of psychology, all coming together according to a careful plan backed by the technical skill and aesthetic inspiration of the artist.

From a distance, good teaching conveys the same naturalness and spontaneity, often leading people to believe that anyone can teach. Close up, however, we see that good teaching requires more than just knowledge of the subject matter. It, too, requires that careful combination of skill and planning, plus a touch of the artist, in order to produce a masterpiece of instruction.

Few of us will ever be the Da Vincis of the classroom, but we can be competent journeymen artists by concentrating on careful planning which takes into account what we are trying to teach, to whom, and under what conditions. This planning process is known as instructional design.

Stated more fully, instructional design involves the following steps, as illustrated in Figure 1.1:

writing instructional objectives;
assessing learner variables, instructor variables, and situational
     constraints;
selecting a teaching method or methods compatible with the ob-
     jectives, learners, and situation and with your strengths as
     an instructor;
sequencing instruction;
incorporating principles derived from learning theory into the
     instruction;
selecting an evaluation method or methods that take into account
     your objectives, the learners, the situation, and your reasons
     for doing the evaluation; and
revising instruction based on the evaluation results.

If this process sounds time-consuming, it is, but so is delivering an ill-conceived instructional unit to students who don't learn the material because the content, presentation, or other aspects were poorly planned. Staff time, then, which is a precious commodity in every library, is better spent up front, in the planning stage, if we are to succeed in conveying our knowledge to students.

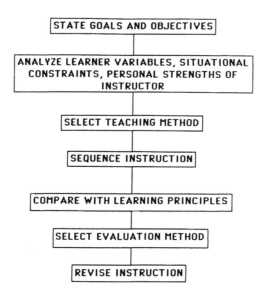

Figure 1.1 Steps in the instructional design process.

With planning as an emphasis, what we present in this volume is not a collection of ideas for action, but rather a discussion of alternatives that are available to you, taking into account the advantages and disadvantages of each. Because every instructional situation is different, an approach that works beautifully with one group of students isn't necessarily appropriate for another. Many variables have to be considered carefully in the planning process. Our goal, then, is to present a process you can use to design instruction wherever you are, just as you hope to impart to students the skills needed to use any library effectively.

We have tried to balance our theoretical framework with an extensive array of examples and a chapter devoted to theory put into action. We begin in Chapter 2 by presenting a model for the analysis of teaching methods that we use throughout this volume. Chapter 3 discusses alternative teaching methods as they fit into this model. We then describe how to choose a teaching method, in Chapter 4. In Chapter 5, we look at ways of using learning theory to enhance instruction once you've chosen your teaching method. Chapter 6 takes the theoretical guidelines covered in the initial chapters and looks at them in practical terms, as we present eight instructional situations often faced by librarians and a description of how each of them could be handled. Chapter 7 discusses the final steps of the process: choosing an evaluation method and using the results to revise instruction. The last chapter summarizes our philosophy about instructional design and, hopefully, inspires you to do likewise.

Before we begin with our model, a point of clarification is in order. Much of the literature of library instruction discusses teaching methods in terms of separate library skills courses versus course-related or course-integrated instruction versus workshops. We consider these alternatives to be instructional *settings* rather than instructional *methods*. The instructional design process can be used in any setting, even though our own bias in many of the examples we give is toward instruction that takes place as part of a course in an academic discipline.

With this definition in mind, let's begin our discussion of teaching methods with the model we present in Chapter 2.

2
A System for Categorizing Instructional Methods

Most of us are aware of several ways of teaching an idea or skill because we have experienced them as the instructor or the student. Asked to name some of these instructional methods, most people would probably list lectures and discussions; some would list films, workbooks, computer-assisted instruction, individual tutoring, and so on. Unfortunately, the list would peter out rapidly because most of us have not been exposed to a wide range of options nor have we thought about the kinds of alternatives which might be available. Even fewer of us have tried to develop new tools; we've been content to teach the way we were taught.

In this chapter and the next, we will look at a wide range of instructional options which could be used alone or in combination to structure a class or other learning sequence. We'll begin by considering an organizational scheme for understanding the structure and function of each type of instruction. Then, using that scheme, we'll examine the various teaching options available to the librarian and how they might be incorporated into teaching.

A MODEL FOR ANALYSIS

All librarians have run into a person who knows how to use only the *Readers' Guide* and, therefore, tries to use it to answer all of his or her information needs. But *Readers' Guide* was not designed to answer all types of questions. That person must realize that different sources deal with information differently, and that the question dictates which source to use. The same is true for teaching methods. The common methods mentioned earlier fit many different teaching situations, but not all. If we continue to think of only those specific methods, we will end up always trying to use one tool to achieve vastly different purposes in widely varying settings.

We would like to take a new perspective on alternative teaching methods, one that recognizes that just as different bibliographic tools have different purposes and approaches, so different instructional tools have different purposes and approaches. When you begin to analyze alternative teaching possibilities in this light, you will be able to go beyond the standard techniques and experiment with some more novel methods. You may even find yourself developing totally new ways to teach your content.

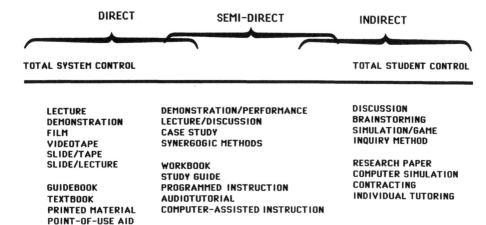

Figure 2.1 A continuum for categorizing instructional methods.

The Direct-to-Indirect Continuum

In this new way of looking at teaching, we analyze instructional methods from the standpoint of who or what determines the sequence of events as the students learn. We call this the *degree of control over learning* and contend that it lies along a continuum as shown in Figure 2.1. At one end of the continuum, the instructor is in total control over what is going on each moment. We call this end of the continuum *direct instruction*. An example of this type of instruction is found in the formal lecture, where the instructor is delivering a prepared text from which he or she does not deviate. Interruptions by the students do not divert the teacher from the planned course, except very briefly. Such total control can also be exercised by something other than a live instructor. For example, a slide/tape can deliver information without interruption just the way a lecturer can. When this is the case, we say that the instructional *system* is in control of the presentation of information and the course of learning.

At the other extreme of the continuum, the *student* is in
total control over what is happening, with only occasional interference from the instructor. We call this end of the continuum
indirect instruction. An example of this type of instruction is the
student-led discussion. The instructor may begin the process by
suggesting a topic for discussion, such as problems students are
having in the library, but from then on it's the students who do
the talking and determine which direction the discussion will take.
The instructor acts as a facilitator and summarizer.

Group vs. Individual Instruction

Lectures and discussions are all forms of group instruction, designed to be presented to several students at once. We can also use
the continuum to understand instruction with one student at a
time. Most point-of-use aids are essentially media-based lectures
given to one person at a time, a form of direct instruction. The
information is presented in a predetermined style and sequence
without regard to differences of the learners. The learner might be
able to skip around or reread parts which were unclear, but there
is usually no provision for active use of the information built into
the presentation.

Further along the continuum toward total student control in
an individual instruction setting is the programmed workbook or
computer-assisted lesson; here student responses control the flow
of instruction. A small amount of information is provided, followed by a question which the student must answer. Correct answers advance the program; incorrect answers return the student
to the original material or supplementary information. As we discuss the control continuum, we will try to provide examples of
both formats, group and individual forms of instruction. The principles governing one will be true for the other most of the time.

TOTAL INSTRUCTOR OR SYSTEM CONTROL: DIRECT INSTRUCTION

Now let's examine what the instructional options look like at each end of the continuum. At the left end, we have those instructional situations exemplifying *total instructor or system control.* The course of instruction can proceed without any input from the students. For the most part, the instructional goal in these instances is the delivery of information or the demonstration of a concept.

In Group Settings

For example, most formal lectures and slide/lectures are designed to give overviews of an area, such as an introduction to the library's services or a description of the organization of the literature in a particular field; they are filled with general ideas and supporting data or examples. The student's role in this situation is to listen and/or watch and absorb the information in a fairly passive manner. Student questions are viewed primarily as digressions from the main purpose of the class period. The object is to cover a certain amount of information in the time allotted. Variations on the straight lecture method are the media-based versions, such as slide/ tapes, videotapes, and so on.

In Individual Settings

The methods just described are all group instructional settings, but the same spirit of one-way instruction is also present in individual instructional settings, where delivery of information is the key purpose and the input of the student is minimal. As mentioned earlier, many point-of-use aids fit this description as do standard textbooks. Most of these methods are designed to deliver information to a single learner without any input from that learner; moreover, the system is not set up to vary according to the needs of the learner.

TOTAL STUDENT CONTROL: INDIRECT INSTRUCTION

At the other end of the continuum we find instructional systems which are totally responsive to the variations of the students. There is still a core of material or skills the students are supposed to be learning, but it is the students and their responses to the activities designed to present that core that determine how the instruction proceeds.

In Group Settings

The best example of a group instructional system of this type is the free-form discussion, known in many quarters as the bull session. Any information conveyed in this setting is incidental; it is the process of discussing that is the focus. A librarian might use this process to air and shape attitudes toward the library and how it functions. Or the librarian may incorporate such a discussion at the end of a formal class period to get the students to suggest other ways they might need to tap the resources of the library.

In Individual Settings

On an individual basis, student control would be represented by one-to-one tutoring such as the type of instruction that would be done at the reference desk in response to a given student's question. In this case, it is the student's questions and responses to the librarian's questions that determine the course of instruction.

AND IN BETWEEN: SEMI-DIRECT INSTRUCTION

In Group Settings

Spanning the distance between these two extremes are all the other possibilities, familiar and unfamiliar, that a librarian might employ. For example, a central position on the continuum is held by the demonstration/performance option, which might be used in teaching users how to do an on-line search. In this case, information and a demonstration are given initially, in order to show the students how their own performance should proceed. This is followed by an opportunity for the students to practice the demonstrated procedure. During this practice time, the librarian moves among the students, correcting errors and providing feedback, all the time monitoring overall student progress. When the practice time is over, the librarian continues the class session by reviewing what was done and using the students' own experiences to highlight problems, provide clarification, and progress toward the next phase of the instruction.

You can see that in this situation the progress of the instruction is determined in part by the preset instructional goals and procedures and in part by the students' own attempts. Group application of these procedures does not allow the instruction to be directed by each individual student's experiences, but takes into account group progress as a whole.

In Individual Settings

In the individual version of this point on the continuum, we would find something like the computer-assisted instructional program we described earlier. These programs begin by providing a small amount of information followed by a question to the student. The student's response then determines what comes next to some extent.

For example, a program to teach students about periodical indexes might begin with a brief description of several indexes and then ask the student which index could probably be used to find information on a given topic. If the student chooses the correct index(es), the program moves on to the next unit. If the student is wrong, the program might explain why the answer chosen was incorrect and give the student a second chance. Although the program determines what material will be presented and, in general, guides the student through the content, it is responsive to student problems and responses.

A FURTHER REFINEMENT

If we consider the various standard teaching options with which we are familiar, we can see that rather than being located at a single point on this continuum, they tend to span a range of values within certain limits. For example, if we analyze what various people call a "lecture," we can see that in some lectures, no student input is present, while for others, students' questions are welcomed and often determine the specific content discussed in the lecture, even though the general topic of the lecture has been decided on by the instructor and he or she does most of the talking.

How far along the continuum could we go before we stopped calling something a lecture? It is unlikely that we could go all the way to the right end of the continuum and still be willing to consider something a lecture. Probably what we understand as a lecture extends only about one third of the way across the continuum before it starts being called a lecture/discussion or question/answer session where students direct questions to the instructor who answers them briefly.

In the same way, what we think of as a discussion has a wide range of possibilities, from the free discussion mentioned earlier to an instructor-controlled discussion which borders on a review session. Generally the discussion concept is one of the exchange of ideas among equals. The more the instructor becomes a dominant figure, the less the class can be considered a discussion.

The various self-instructional methods with which we are familiar also span the continuum. Point-of-use aids tend to fall at the end of the continuum because their primary purpose is to deliver information on the use of a particular tool. They do not as a rule require any active responding from the learner, but simply lead the learner step by step through a process. They are not set up to respond to learner input such as questions or errors. If the learner makes an error, there is no mechanism for guiding him or her back to the correct path.

Part way across the continuum we would find materials such as audiotutorial systems or workbooks, which provide some information and then have the student respond to a few questions such as, "Write the name of an example of an index here." No feedback is given, and the program continues on regardless of whether or not the student actually wrote a correct example or anything at all. Other types of programs, such as computer-assisted tutorials and programmed texts, are designed to give feedback on the correctness of the student's response. A learner is provided information, asked a question, and given immediate feedback on the accuracy of the response. Some programs are designed to give remediation at that point if the response is incorrect.

The more the progress of the program is determined by the learner's answers, the further to the right on the continuum the program lies. Farthest to the right of individual instruction options is probably the computer simulation of a search process in which students can ask the computer to test what would happen to our list of possibilities if we combined terms in category A with those in category B. Here the student is in total control of what comes next.

The model just discussed should give you a feeling for the ways instruction can be varied according to the needs of the situation. In a later chapter, we will see how those various considerations shape which option we choose and how we mix and match options to structure a class period or learning system. For simplicity's sake, however, let's divide the continuum into three overlapping divisions. We have labeled them direct instruction, semidirect instruction, and indirect instruction, to reflect the degree to which the instructional system controls the coverage of the material. In the following chapter, we examine the major characteristics of each in an effort to determine which type fits which situation and how we can maximize the efficiency of each.

3
Major Subdivisions of the Continuum

DIRECT INSTRUCTION

General Description

In direct instruction, the goal is the transmission of information from a source to the students, individually or as a group. Information flow is primarily one way with very little participation on the part of the learner other than listening, watching, and absorbing. The organization of the content is done by whoever or whatever is presenting it, most of the activity which occurs during the instruction is by the presenter, and the focus of attention is the presenter.

Group Systems

Lecture

The prototype direct instructional system used with groups is the lecture. In the lecture, the information is being delivered to a group of students by the instructor, using his or her organization at his or her pace. The task of the students is to listen carefully, take notes if necessary, and extract the main points. It is the instructor who is in control of the class and who decides what will happen and when and how.

Demonstration

The demonstration is a lecture which illustrates a procedure or principle. The instructor performs the procedure, highlighting each step. Librarians frequently use this procedure when they explain to a class how to use a particular reference tool. Students are not given an opportunity to try the procedure themselves during class, although they may be expected to have learned enough to carry it out on their own later. Demonstrations may also be used to illustrate a concept, such as what a librarian does when conducting a computer data base search. The students are not expected to learn how to do the search, but rather to appreciate what is involved.

Film, Videotape, Slide/Tape

These three options are simply the automated versions of the lecture or demonstration. Instead of having a live instructor present the information, it is presented in a mediated format. These media versions may include more interesting visual material and greater visual diversity than a traditional lecture and may be able to present a wider range of content, but information still is being delivered in a one-way mode.

Slide/Lecture

This very common direct instructional option is also simply a media-based version of the formal lecture or demonstration. Information flow is one way, and the students are passive recipients while the instructor does most of the work.

Individual Systems

Book or Printed Material

The prototype direct instructional system for the individual is the guidebook, which has short prose descriptions of points of interest or procedures, similar to the kind used for tourists. A more familiar and complicated academic alternative would be the textbook or other printed material. As in the lecture, there is a single, organized delivery of information which does not require any active responding on the part of the learners other than reading. If you've ever watched some students with their textbooks, you can see just how passive they are. They allow the words to simply flow by them, just as in a lecture they allow the instructor's words to flow by them without registering. Students can skip around in printed material and reread what was unclear, but the material remains immutable.

Point-of-Use Guide

The very familiar point-of-use aids are often the media version of the individual direct system. While some are in a printed format, in many the information is delivered by slide/tape or videotape without requiring much from the learner other than listening and looking.

Advantages of Direct Instruction

In addition to being the type of instruction with which most students are familiar and, therefore, most comfortable, this type of instruction has some definite advantages. For example, most students already have many of the skills necessary to learn from direct instruction, simply because they have had so much practice with it. They have learned how to listen to lectures, to respond to visual and verbal cues about what is important and what is not. This won't be true for all students, however, and even the best students occasionally have difficulty with poorly presented material.

Direct instruction also has the advantage of being very time conserving. One instructor can "deliver" a lot of information in a very small amount of time, a frequently found situation. We must remember, however, that one cannot equate delivery of information with learning of that information.

With direct instruction, the instructor can maintain very tight control over what information is presented and how it is presented. This allows for very good organization of a presentation, which facilitates learning. The instructor can be certain that all the necessary information is presented and in an order which will make it maximally clear to most students.

Direct instruction is particularly useful for giving overviews of large areas of content, for example, the scheme by which the contents of most indexes are organized. Such overviews make later learning more efficient because they provide an organizational structure into which subsequent details can be fit. Once the students have an overview on how indexes are organized, they can approach each individual index using that overview to guide their use of it.

In some cases, material that is not available in any other format can be presented in a lecture. This is particularly true in areas that are changing constantly. For example, the lag between the initiation of a new service or tool and a readily available printed description of it can often be quite long. Or the material available about a particular tool might be aimed at an audience of professional librarians and would be useless for a group of beginning students. Or the individual library's approach to a particular program might be very different from that generally taken. In these instances, lectures can bridge the gap between need and availability of information.

Finally, an enthusiastic presentation of the material can be very motivating for students. If the speaker is particularly dynamic or a film very well done, students can be excited and challenged to delve more deeply into the material on their own. Sometimes this is the actual objective of the presentation: to inspire the listeners to try something new or to seek the assistance of the librarians, who are not such bad people after all.

Disadvantages of Direct Instruction

On the other hand, there are some distinct learning disadvantages from this type of instruction. The most critical problem is that not everyone can learn at the same pace or from the same materials. The regimentation of most direct instructional methods creates problems for students for whom the presentation style is not immediately clear. Most direct instruction is not responsive to individual differences among the students. This is particularly a problem in group settings where a confused student cannot stop the presentation and have the message repeated. At least in textbooks and guidebooks, the student can reread the material, even though there is no guarantee it will be any clearer the second or third time through.

A second but more subtle difficulty with direct instruction is the underlying message, intentional or unintentional, that there *is* a correct way of viewing the content and that the instructor is the source of that correct viewpoint. This is particularly evident in students who unquestioningly accept what is printed in their texts. They have not learned to trust their own abilities to learn and question. Since we know that there are many ways to approach an information problem, we may be defeating our own purposes if we communicate this message of one correct way, however subtly. Once a learner begins to think that there is a "correct" way to do things, he or she becomes less confident and willing to explore, for fear of making errors. Such a rigid approach to learning might deprive the learner of some very valuable information or keep him or her from learning new ways of doing things.

Finally, because information flow is generally in one direction from the instructor to the students, direct instruction provides little opportunity for active student participation in learning. As we'll see in the chapter on learning theory, students need to use the information presented or practice the skill demonstrated while instruction is still in progress so they can test their understanding of the material and receive instructor feedback on the accuracy of their responses. We'll go into this concept in more depth when we discuss semi-direct instruction, where the opportunity for responding is an important component of the system.

SEMI-DIRECT INSTRUCTION

General Description

In this type of instruction, the goal is to present students with information and then have them use that information in some task during or immediately following instruction. Therefore, this type of instruction is used to teach applications, processes, problem solving, and other practical concepts. The students' efforts are orchestrated by the instructor or other instructional source. The outcome of the students' efforts will be fairly predictable. The course of instruction does not depend on the students' responses, but rather is predetermined by the instructor. The students first listen to or read the information needed to accomplish the task and then are guided through the task by instructions or questions given by the instructor.

The instructor's role in semi-direct instruction is to set up the initial presentation, demonstration, case, or reading material in such a way that the students can use the information readily. The instructor is also responsible for setting up the task the students will engage in to test their understanding of the initial presentation. In some versions of semi-direct instruction, the instructor's task is to test student understanding through questions which follow the initial presentation. Finally, the instructor must assess overall student progress in order to provide a summary of the lesson and to determine the pace at which to continue the instruction.

The student's role in this type of instruction is more active than in direct instruction. The student must make careful observations as the content or model is presented, extract from it the critical information, and reproduce that content or skill in a new setting during the practice time. Much of what the students do in this type of instruction is analyze and apply the concepts which are explained by the instructor or material to shape their own response.

Group Systems

Demonstration/Performance
The prototype semi-direct group instruction would be the demonstration/performance. Demonstration/performance is primarily used in teaching skills or processes that are done in steps. In this format the instruction begins with an overview of the task the students are going to learn, accompanied by an expert example of the performance. Then the students attempt to copy the model themselves. The instructor circulates and provides immediate feedback

on how they're doing. Once everyone has had a chance to try the task, the instructor summarizes what went on and makes some general comments about the performances.

For example, a librarian might demonstrate to the entire group how to use the OCLC terminal to locate a particular book for interlibrary loan by using a terminal and an overhead projection system which allows everyone to see what is on the screen. Then groups of three students follow the same procedures on their terminals to locate a different book. The students follow the librarian's steps, substituting the title or author or other information provided to them by the librarian. As they work, the librarian circulates and answers questions and makes comments.

The instructor's role in this type of instruction is to provide a good model or good initial coverage of the necessary material so that the students can experience success when they are given the opportunity to try their hand at applying it. The instructor must also be available to assist the students as they attempt to replicate the sample performance. Finally, the instructor summarizes after the performance phase and ties up any loose ends.

Lecture/Discussion
In this form of semi-direct instruction, the initial presentation of material is followed by a question-and-answer period. During the latter phase, questions can go in either direction; the students may ask about things that were unclear in the presentation, or the instructor may use questions to determine how well the students understood the presentation. It is through these questions and through the initial emphasis on the material that the instructor controls the progress of material coverage. There is some responsiveness to the students' needs because student questions and their responses to instructor questions will determine how much review

or additional coverage will be included. Just about any kind of material that doesn't involve the application of a process can be taught in this format.

Case Study

This is a more unusual form of semi-direct instruction. It is used mostly when the goal of instruction is teaching processes, analysis, or evaluation. In this system, students are given the case, which is a description of a problem situation and how it was resolved, to read and analyze. Occasionally this analysis is preceded by an explanation of a process one can use to analyze what is going on in a case. After the students have had a chance to pick the case apart on their own or in small groups, the instructor begins asking questions about the case which are designed to bring out the main points it makes. The questions might be, "What different events occurred during the course of this incident?" or "What assumptions did the main person in this case make about the availability of resources?" The students respond to those questions based on what they found in the case description. They are also free to ask questions about details and processes which might be operating. Once the case has been thoroughly analyzed and, sometimes, the actions evaluated, the instructor summarizes the analysis and evaluation and comments on how acceptable the final analysis was and why.

A librarian might use a case study to explore with a class how well a particular fictitious student documented a research paper. For example, the students would be given a description of the assignment which the fictional student was attempting and a copy of the outline of the student's paper with notes indicating what reference sources were used where. Some of the points of the paper would have no reference backup; others would have references from inappropriate or biased sources. The students would be asked to evaluate how well the student had used reference sources in the plan of the paper. One can see that this would have to be a fairly sophisticated audience. A simpler version might take a fictitious student through an information search in the library, having him or her take several wrong turns while moving from reference source to reference source. Students could analyze the search and find places where wrong sources were used and so on.

In some versions of semi-direct instruction, the instructor prepares materials which will take groups of students through the material without direct intervention by the instructor. Several of these group methods are discussed by Mouton and Blake (1984) in the process they call *synergogy*, the cooperative learning within a group.

Team-Effectiveness
The first of Mouton and Blake's methods, called "team effectiveness," has the class divided into small groups of four or five. The instructor has the students read some material about the content to be learned. Each student individually takes an objectively-scorable test over this material; then students in each group cooperate to take the test together. The correct answers are handed out when the group tests are over, and the group and individual tests are scored. The group score is almost always higher than any individual test score because each group member contributes to the overall knowledge base. In producing group responses to the structured tests, the students actively participate, receive feedback on their understanding, and learn from one another. An instructor may not wish to use this as the sole teaching method, but may follow it up with a review of the most commonly missed items or confusing questions, done in a lecture/discussion format.

A librarian might use team effectiveness as an alternative to an introductory "Here's the Library" lecture. The librarian could provide the students with a description of the library, its services, and layout. Each student would take a short quiz asking where things are, who does what, and how to do a few things, all in a multiple-choice format. Then the students would work together in small groups to answer the questions by pooling their responses. Once the team has completed their composite test, they are given the correct answers and instructed to score their own tests as well as the team's test. Recognition is given to that team achieving the highest composite score.

Attitude Clarification

A related technique can be used to explore students' attitudes. In this method, instead of answering multiple-choice questions about factual material, the students are given problem situations which reflect certain values or attitudes; students indicate how similar various response choices are to their own attitudes. Then the small groups work together to try to select the most reasoned attitude of the alternatives. Once they have some consensus on their choices, the instructor gives them a "correct" response sheet, that is, a sheet indicating what the most reasoned responses would be; students go back and compare their choices with the "correct" choices and discuss them once again.

This type of procedure might be used to help students understand why they should treat library materials with care, what plagiarism is, or why certain library rules are made. For example, the questions on the survey might be examples of different behaviors commonly seen in the library and would ask the student how serious a problem such a behavior is and why. Group discussion would then bring out different student attitudes about appropriate behavior and at least force the students to explore their own attitudes.

Team-Member Teach

Another of Mouton and Blake's methods is a student-teach-student design called "team-member teaching." Once again the instructor sets up the task by providing each student with some material to read, but in this case each group member gets a different topic to become familiar with. Afterward, each team member is required to "teach" the others on the team the essence of what that member has just learned from his or her particular reading. Once the "teaching" phase is completed, the other team members take a multiple-choice test over all the material to see how well both "students" and "teachers" have done. They are given the correct answers and allowed to score their own tests; they then review missed items with the team member responsible for "teaching" that concept.

A librarian might use this model to familiarize students with several different types of reference tools. Each student in a group would be responsible for summarizing the information about a different tool and explaining that tool to his or her colleagues.

Performance-Judging

Another of Mouton and Blake's models which can be very useful is called the "performance judging" design and is generally employed when trying to teach skills or evaluative abilities. In this situation, students work in groups and begin by attempting to identify the characteristics of an effective example of whatever skill they are learning. The group then compares the criteria they selected with that offered by the expert. They then apply those criteria to their own performance. This technique is helpful in getting students to understand and accept evaluative criteria.

For example, a librarian might be trying to teach students what makes a good bibliography. In groups, they would attempt to list the characteristics of a good bibliography themselves. Once they have their lists, they are given a list compiled by experts; the groups compare their own lists with that of the authoritative source, looking for commonalities and discrepancies and trying to understand why any differences exist. They then use the experts' list to evaluate their own bibliographies.

Individual Systems

For individual instruction, semi-direct methods involve instructional materials which guide the student through the material but require the student to make active responses to questions or problems posed in the course of covering the material.

Workbook, Study Guide, and Programmed Instruction

These three types of semi-direct instruction represent different points on the continuum, but all deal with instruction through printed material. The instructor controls the learning through the order of presentation and the types of activities demanded of the student, but the students are working on their own.

The most familiar individual form of semi-direct instruction is the workbook. Workbooks generally consist of small segments of information followed by a series of questions or exercises which the student is required to complete. The analogy to the demonstration/performance group method is obvious: Information is provided, and the student must use that information in an exercise. The degree to which these exercises are monitored and feedback given on the correctness of the student's response varies, but generally there is some attempt in these materials to provide the student with some indication of how he or she is progressing.

A more active and directed version of the workbook is the study guide. While most workbooks incorporate student activities at the end of a section of material, study guides tend to have directions to the student throughout the text. Questions at the beginning of a unit direct the student's attention to what is to be covered, questions are included throughout the text, and the unit ends with a specific task to be completed. The study guide format incorporates much more activity. One might imagine it sitting further to the right on the active student-control continuum than the workbook.

A slightly more sophisticated version of the workbook and study guide is the programmed-instruction text. In these materials the actual progress through the content is contingent on student responses. In linear programmed texts each small concept is followed by a question which the student must answer. That answer is then followed by the correct answer, against which the student can compare his or her answer. Every student reads all the material and responds to each question, thus moving through the material in a linear fashion. In a branched programmed text, the material the student sees and the direction he or she goes next depend on the responses made to the questions. Correct answers pass the student on to new material; incorrect answers return the student for extra work on the points missed.

All of the above methods can be used to teach similar content. The primary differences among them have to do with how often and when the student is required to respond during the presentation of material. One might imagine a librarian designing some instruction on the use of various indexes, using these three different formats. In the workbook format, each index would be described separately, followed by a series of questions which the student would have to answer using the index in question. The workbook might end up with a section on comparative use of the indexes and an exercise on evaluating the appropriateness of each index for various topics.

A study guide designed to do the same task might begin with a brief case description of an information problem asking the students to indicate the kinds of information that the individual in question needs. This section would be intended to alert the student to the fact that there are differences in the types of information a person might need and that the process of finding additional information might depend on what one already has. Then each of the indexes would be examined in that context. An index might be introduced by selecting one of the information types needed. Through a series of brief descriptions and questions, the student would examine the index in an attempt to locate the information in question. After all indexes were examined, the study guide would probably end with the same type of consolidating exercise as the workbook.

A programmed text on this material could take either presentation sequence. Its distinguishing feature would be the frequency of questions asked of the student and the speed with which the student would learn the correctness of the answers.

Audiotutorial Instruction
The media-based version of the workbook is the audiotutorial module. In this case the information or model is presented in some visual medium such as a slide/tape or videotape and is accompanied by a workbook in which the student performs periodic exercises as necessary. This differs from the point-of-use slide/tape described earlier in that audiotutorials have active student response as an integral part of their structure.

Computer-Assisted Instruction
A more sophisticated version of the audiotutorial and the programmed text is computer-assisted instruction (CAI). In this format, the computer is used to present information to the student and to ask questions and evaluate answers. Most CAI programs have a branching capability built in, which allows the student to be routed to material based on the correctness of his or her re-

sponses to the periodic questions. As computers became more sophisticated and efficient, CAI programs added more and more capabilities for individualizing instruction. Researchers are now working on intelligent computer-assisted instruction programs which will be able to "follow" a student's logic in answering a question and tailor the course of instruction even more closely to the way that student learns best. These programs will be almost as responsive to the student as a human tutor might be.

Librarians can use CAI programs to do anything that programmed texts or audiotutorials can do, unless there is a need to use the actual reference sources or other library tools. In some cases, these materials can be simulated on the computer through drawings, but if the real sources are readily available, reason and learning theory dictate using them as much as possible. Restrictions on CAI use are primarily practical rather than instructional.

Advantages of Semi-Direct Instruction

The semi-direct methods have the big advantage over direct methods of incorporating active student responding into the instruction. As we'll see later, this has some real benefits for both students and instructor. For the students, opportunities for active participation result in much better understanding of what is learned because it forces them into a deeper and different processing of information than does passive reception. It also provides the students with an opportunity to receive direct feedback on how the learning is progressing before it's too late. Instruction incorporating active participation also promotes the transferability of the learning from the classroom to real-life situations.

Semi-direct methods allow the instructor to maintain control over the direction the instruction will take. This control makes planning easier. Semi-direct methods also provide the instructor with feedback on how instruction is progressing so that adjustments can be made.

Disadvantages of Semi-Direct Instruction

One problem with semi-direct methods is that they are more time consuming than direct methods, both in and out of class. In class, time must be set aside for student practice in demonstration/performance. In case studies and instructor-led discussions, student responses are often inaccurate or insufficient, requiring time for correction. Or they are slow in coming, requiring patience from the instructor and the other students. Outside of class, the instructor must devote more time to preparation so that questions, instructions, and other materials are clear to the students. The instructor also needs to anticipate some of the turns which student responding might take and be prepared to deal with them.

For students, semi-direct methods present a different problem. Many of them have never been exposed to these methods before, and their learning skills are not adapted to the situation. As we'll discuss later, an important learning skill for these methods is the ability to summarize and extract main points and generalizations from an excess of information, some relevant, some not. Unfortunately, many students have difficulty with this skill; therefore, it falls on the instructor to provide summaries and consolidations of what has gone on in class.

INDIRECT INSTRUCTION

General Description

We have now reached the end of the continuum where most of the attention is focused on student-directed learning. The instructor's role changes to that of facilitator and summarizer, while the students do much of the thinking, analyzing, and learning. The goal of these methods is to have the students discover the concepts or apply what they've learned in new and different situations without a lot of intervention from the instructor. This type of instruction is best used when students are learning application, analysis, and evaluation.

Group Systems

Discussion

The prototype indirect group method is the discussion. In a discussion class, students express their solutions, opinions, and ideas; defend them against attack; compare them with those of their classmates; and, through that process, come to some consensus which hopefully approximates what the instructor would have said in a lecture on the topic. The instructor initiates the discussion, usually with a question or provocative statement, and then uses questions or brief comments to guide the discussion indirectly. The instructor also summarizes the discussion periodically to help students identify major points and issues which have been raised.

A librarian might use discussion to have students suggest ways they have used in the past to locate a particular type of information or how they feel about a variety of library policies or what constitutes inappropriate use of resource material.

Brainstorming

As with most other methods, there are degrees of indirect instruction, and so discussions can vary from very structured to very unstructured, such as brainstorming. Brainstorming is a type of discussion intended to stimulate creative thinking and problem solving. Brainstorming discussions seldom last more than ten minutes. The instructor poses a problem or asks a question, and the students begin to throw out ideas and suggestions as they occur to them. These ideas are written on the board without any comment from the instructor or other students. The purpose is to raise as many ideas as possible for a more structured discussion later. Once the flow of ideas has stopped, the instructor switches to a different type of discussion or to small-group work to evaluate the ideas which have been suggested.

A librarian might use brainstorming to generate paper topics centering around a particular broad topic or to list all the possible sources one could use to locate information on a particular topic or all the different categories under which a particular book could be filed if one were trying to understand the cataloging system.

Simulation and Game
While discussion teaching has many uses, a more effective instructional method at this end of the continuum is the simulation or the game. There is some disagreement about the degree to which these two are related, but any real difference between them is procedural. From a learning standpoint, they are very similar. In both games and simulations, the students are placed in a situation which simulates a real problem-solving setting, and they must either apply a process they have learned or discover the process by analyzing what happens during the simulation. The former is a simpler task since the latter requires that the student be able to solve the problem and discover the process at the same time. This two-level requirement is often beyond lower-level students. The instructor sets up the simulation, providing materials that describe the situation, and then allows the students to manipulate the simulation to reach some predetermined goal.

For example, in a city-planning class the instructor might divide the class into groups and assign each group a different role in city government or politics. One group might be the city council, another group the planning commission, another group the developer interests, a fourth group neighborhood activists. They might be given the problem of locating an area in the city for a park. The group representing the city council must vote on where to locate the park; the other groups try to convince the council to locate it where they want it. These interest groups must marshal evidence and arguments to support their positions. Once the evidence has been presented and the council has made its decision, the instructor conducts a debriefing in which the class reviews what went on in the simulation and critiques the performance of the various groups.

Most of the instructor's time goes into the development of the simulation, the explanation to the students, and the debriefing at the end. There is no "correct" outcome of a simulation or a game. It is the process that is important rather than the product.

A librarian could use simulations to teach a variety of processes, such as the process for topic narrowing. John Kupersmith of the University of Texas has used just such a procedure very successfully. First, students are shown how to take a very general topic and, by placing on it a series of restrictions such as time span, place, people involved, and so on, generate many different topics for papers. Then he has the class as a group select a very broad topic, such as television. The class is divided into small groups, and each group applies the narrowing process to that broad topic, simulating what would be done in real life. Each group ends up with a topic statement, all of which are then put up on the board and compared. This procedure very successfully illustrates how one can narrow a research paper topic and come up with a wide range of potential papers from the same general topic.

Inquiry Method
A similar process is being employed in the inquiry method. In this situation, students are required to observe and manipulate a set of objects or data and discover whatever underlying principle they

represent. The students essentially repeat the process of discovery that experts have gone through. For example, students in physics labs are given string, weights, and rulers. Eventually, through playing around with these items, they can make some observations about the relationship of weight and swing to pendulum motion and from there to some of the more basic laws of physics. For the most part, the instructor does not intervene, except to provide the initial materials, answer questions during the observation period, and conduct a debriefing after the students have come to their conclusions.

A librarian might find such a procedure useful in helping students understand how books are cataloged. For example, each group of students might be given a stack of books (or cards representing books), complete with call numbers, tables of contents, authors' names, and so on, and asked to make some observations about these books and how they are similar and different. After some time spent examining the books, the librarian could ask the groups to sort their books in some order and then explain their system to the others. The systems they generate could then be compared with the real cataloging system.

Individual Systems

Research Paper

Perhaps the most indirect method we have for teaching library use is the research paper itself. The theory behind research papers is that going through the process of preparing such a paper will teach students all they need to know about library use at this time. In this method's purest form, there is almost no intervention in the learning process by the instructor; students are usually left on their own to discover the alternative ways of doing research. However, it is very seldom that we see a completely self-directed instruction even with the research paper. Most instructors feel the necessity to provide some guidance to the students, even though it is often minimal. To make this type of self-instruction more effective, the instructor should include something like a diary, in which students can introspect on the processes they are going through in the production of the paper. Or the instructor may divide the full-blown paper into several chunks or steps and provide feedback on student progress at each step.

Computer Simulation
Computer simulations which allow a student to manipulate variables and predict outcomes are becoming more and more common as technology becomes more sophisticated. In computer simulations, the instructor has programmed the computer with a model of the real world that will generate answers to questions put to it depending on the values of certain variables. For example, in psychology a simulation might be of a patient in a diagnostic interview. The student would ask the "patient" questions and the computer would provide the most probable answer, based on a given diagnosis. The student's task is to determine what the diagnosis would be. Each time the student runs the program, he or she could be confronted with a different "patient" with different symptoms, generated on a probabilistic basis by the computer. This is only one type of simulation which is possible.

It would seem very natural for someone to be able to develop a computer program that would allow simulation of the information-searching process. For example, the student could be instructed to locate information on the effects of rainfall (or lack of it) on a certain group of people in Africa. The student would go to the computer and ask to see a particular reference tool from a specified list to begin the process of gathering information, such as looking in the *Readers' Guide* under "rain." The computer would respond by indicating the type of information that would be available in that resource. From there the student could call up different tools.

The object of the simulation would be to find the information using the fewest tools or the fewest steps in searching. The computer could even provide prompts or hints in case the student ends up in a blind alley.

Contracting

Perhaps a better way of referring to this method would be individual problem solving or even tutoring, although the latter title implies more individual attention than is often possible. In contracting instruction, the individual student creates a set of learning goals and ways of reaching these goals in conjunction with the instructor. Some of the goals may come from the instructor's predetermined set of minimum criteria for learning; others come from the individual student's interests and projects. The student and instructor then work together to lay out a method for achieving these goals and a timeline within which the goals can be achieved. The student then proceeds to work alone, occasionally checking back with the instructor when problems arise. The instructor allows the student to lead the interaction and serves primarily as a resource and facilitator rather than a direct source of instruction. Once the goals have been achieved, the student returns to the instructor with evidence of the achievement to be evaluated.

This type of instruction may be a very formal written contract, or it may exist only as an interaction between the instructor and the student, as in an individual question-and-answer session at the reference desk. Whatever its form, the key features are the student-directed nature of the work and the preset goals and procedures for attaining those goals agreed on by the student and instructor.

The closest type of library instruction to this would probably be done at the reference desk, as mentioned earlier, or in the context of a class period as a supplement to other instruction. For example, a librarian may work with a group of graduate students on applying general principles of search strategies to their dissertation work. Since each student will be so different in topic and area, the general principles will have to be tailored to each student's needs. This can be done by first offering the general model and then allowing time for the students to attempt to modify it for their own purposes, which the librarian then reviews individually with each student.

Advantages of Indirect Instruction

Obviously, of the three major divisions of instruction, the indirect instructional methods offer the greatest opportunities for active student participation. Therefore, all the benefits described for semi-direct methods apply here as well. One difference which could be a problem is that, in general, indirect methods have a greater delay in feedback on students' responses than the semi-direct methods. This delay can lead to problems and confusion unless the instructor is careful to provide a thorough review of the students' experience at the end.

Perhaps the greatest advantage of these methods is their ability to allow the students to accept more responsibility for their own learning. When they experience success, they become more confident in their own abilities to learn, feeling less need to have the instructor give them "the answer." This is a particularly useful attitude to develop in students who must learn to function on their own in the library.

Disadvantages of Indirect Instruction

Perhaps the biggest problem with indirect methods is their unpredictability. By their very nature, these methods follow the students through their exploration of a topic. Because each student's learning processes are different, the direction a lesson will take cannot always be anticipated. Therefore, the instructor must be very flexible and capable of responding to any situation that arises. This requires a very thorough knowledge of the subject or a good ability to "think on your feet." It also requires a great deal of self-confidence in one's ability to handle any situation that might arise.

An additional disadvantage of these methods is similar to one in the semi-direct mode: the students' lack of experience in learning from this type of situation. The skills needed to benefit from a discussion are quite different from those which are used in learning from a lecture. They require quite a bit of sophistication on the part of the student, in order to be able to simultaneously participate, monitor main points, and process ideas. Therefore, instructors have to bear the burden of seeing to it that the content of the indirect instruction is summarized and consolidated for the students or possibly teach the students how to do this for themselves.

Another extremely large problem with indirect methods is the time they require. These methods take longer than any other instructional method. One must be sure that the benefits gained from devoting this much class time to one activity will outweigh the time lost to other forms of instruction.

IN SUMMARY

From the foregoing discussion, you can see that there are several options for teaching open to you. No one method fits all situations and no one situation fits all methods. In fact, it is most often the case that more than one method will be used in a single class session. For example, the class may begin with a discussion of problems students are anticipating, followed by a short lecture which ties the problems identified by the students to people and resources within the library which can be used to find solutions to those problems. This could then lead into a case study or simulation to illustrate how a student can tap into the resources just identified. The class could close with individual planning time in which each student works out a system for dealing with his or her individual problem.

Another example might be in teaching a class session on proper use of reference sources in preparing a paper. The librarian might begin with a team-effectiveness task, having the students read and evaluate a short paper in which there are some glaring examples of poorly used references, first individually and then as a group. Then the librarian could give a brief lecture reviewing effective use of sources, followed by another team-effectiveness task of the same type, but with a new paper.

This mixing and matching of instruction has many advantages. The variety makes the class more interesting and usually gets the students more involved. By using different methods, an instructor touches more of the students because not all students learn equally well in the same manner. And not all instructors are equally facile at all types of instruction, so a little variety keeps you from struggling through a class session using a single method with which you aren't comfortable.

It is also possible that now that you have seen what some of the possibilities are, you will begin to design variations on these options. They are by no means the only possibilities; they are just some suggestions. By reflecting on the model of the continuum, you may discover that there are many variations on the methods just presented. By all means explore them.

The question that now faces us, however, is how to decide which method to choose. The next chapter will offer some suggestions about the variables that are important in making an instructional choice.

REFERENCE

Mouton, J. S., and Blake, R. R. (1984). *Synergogy: A New Strategy for Education, Training, and Development*, Jossey-Bass, Inc., Publishers, San Francisco.

4
Designing and Sequencing Instruction

DESIGNING AN INSTRUCTIONAL UNIT

In the previous chapter, we saw that as an instructor, you have many options available to you; you could probably design even more options with a little creativity. In this chapter, we intend to lay out a model for designing an instructional unit which will allow you to choose among the alternatives and sequence them for maximum instructional benefit.

Let's begin by examining how to choose among the various types of instruction just enumerated. There are four main factors to consider in the selection of an instructional method or methods:

1. the objectives or content
2. the students
3. the situation
4. the instructor

We have listed them in order of importance, recognizing that each subsequent category can modify the choices dictated by the previous categories.

The Objectives or Content

From the previous chapter we already have some hint of how the objectives of instruction determine the choice of method. In discussing our three main categories of methods, we emphasized that they serve different purposes. Direct instruction is primarily for inspiring or informing the students; semi-direct instruction works best when used to teach a skill or process; indirect instruction can be used to give students practice in application, to allow them to discover information, or to motivate them to learn. Immediately, we can see that the objective of the instruction will weigh in favor of one of these methods over another.

To put this in more conventional educational terms, we would refer to the three types of educational objectives outlined by Bloom (1956):

Cognitive (informational or intellectual skills)
Affective (inspirational or attitudinal)
Psychomotor (physical skills)

Cognitive objectives can be broken down even further into the following:

Basic objectives—knowledge or comprehension of facts or concepts. Example: Students can describe the purpose of using *Readers' Guide*.

Intermediate objectives—application of facts or concepts to new
    situations. Example: Students can locate a topic in *Readers'
    Guide*.
Advanced objectives—analysis of situations, synthesis of new
    models, evaluation of facts and ideas. Example: Students can
    decide whether or not to use *Readers' Guide* for a given
    question.

Affective objectives can be broken down into the following
categories:

Basic objectives—simple awareness of the issue. Example: Stu-
    dents can describe the proper use of references in a paper
    and why they are appropriate.
Intermediate objectives—willingness to comply with an issue.
    Example: Students will correctly cite references in their
    written work, based on externally stated rules.
Advanced objectives—analysis and establishment of a personal
    value system with regard to the issue. Example: Students
    will describe and defend their own evaluations of a given
    use of references.

Psychomotor objectives would not be broken down for most
library instruction. An example of a psychomotor objective for
library instruction would be that the student would insert a microfiche into a reader correctly. At this level, most psychomotor objectives have cognitive components as well. For example, in addition to inserting the microfiche into the reader, the student would
have to know how to position it upright, how to search the pages,
and so on, in addition to the physical act of manipulating the
equipment.

All instructional design must begin with the specification of
the objectives of the instruction, a fact well known to most librarians. These objectives need to be specified in terms of the

change which will take place in the student as a function of the instruction. For these reasons, objectives are usually phrased as "the student will be able to" or "the student will do" some particular thing. These statements are *not* descriptions of what will happen in class. For example, "The student will participate in a discussion on the symbolism in Goethe's *Faust*" is *not* an instructional objective; it is a description of the instructional method. The objective would be phrased in terms of what the student got out of that discussion of Goethe; for example, "The student will be able to analyze any passage from *Faust* in terms of the symbolism used" or "The student will be able to list the forms of symbolism used in Goethe's *Faust*." Some examples of objectives for library instruction might be the following:

Cognitive

   Basic

The student will describe the services offered by the branch libraries.

The student will list the indexes available in his or her particular field of study.

The student will list the steps to follow in searching for a reference.

   Intermediate

The student will locate on a map of the library the place where each item on a list of sources would be found.

The student will use the OCLC terminal to determine if a given book is owned by the library.

The student will create a specific paper topic, given a general topic, by using a topic narrowing procedure.

   Advanced

The student will describe a potential search strategy to answer a specific question.

The student will evaluate the appropriateness of a set of reference
sources for a given paper topic.

The student will create a set of cross-referenced index cards for a
set of references pertaining to a dissertation topic.

Affective

Basic

The student can repeat library regulations on the care of library
materials.

The student can describe why a certain regulation exists.

The student can describe how a search strategy makes topic-
searching more efficient.

The student identifies the library as a possible source of assistance for information questions.

Intermediate

The student abides by library regulations on the care of materials.

The student uses an efficient search strategy whenever researching
a topic.

The student approaches librarians for assistance when problems
arise.

Advanced

The student develops several alternate strategies for making use of
the library's resources.

The student keeps informed of new reference tools as they
become available.

Psychomotor

The student can operate the various pieces of equipment in the
library, such as the microfiche/microfilm readers, computer
terminals, and audiovisual equipment.

If we consider the various types of objectives listed above and
how they fit with the types of instruction discussed in the previous

CONSTRAINT	DIRECT	SEMI-DIRECT	INDIRECT
Objective			
Cognitive			
basic	+	—	—
intermediate	—	+	0
advanced	—	0	+
Affective			
basic	+	0	+
intermediate	+	+	+
advanced	—	0	+
Psychomotor	—	+	0

(Legend: **+** = recommend; **0** = acceptable; **—** = don't recommend)

	DIRECT	SEMI-DIRECT	INDIRECT
Students			
Background	little	some	a lot
Learning Skills	little	some	a lot
Situation			
Time	not much needed	more needed	a lot needed
Class size	medium to large	small to medium	small to medium
Classroom	standard	some flexibility	much flexibility
Resources	possibly media	depends on type	usually nothing
Instructor	speaking	questioning	organizing/design
	conceptualizing	giving feedback	facilitating
	enthusiasm	demonstrating	summarizing
	using media	presenting	listening
	organizing	monitoring progress	patience
	"reading" audience	patience	flexibility
			self-control

Figure 4.1   Criteria for matching instructional methods to variables.

chapter, we would come up with a chart like Figure 4.1. It compares the usefulness of our three main instructional categories with the three main types of objectives and their subtypes. For example, we can see that direct instruction is useful for achieving basic cognitive objectives (that is, knowledge at fairly factual levels) and basic affective objectives (that is, inspiring students to become aware of a given issue), but not good at all for psychomotor objectives. On the other hand, semi-direct instruction is particularly good for giving students practice in intermediate cognitive objectives (application skills), only moderately useful for most affective objectives, but very useful for psychomotor objectives, such as having students use a piece of equipment, usually taught by demonstration/performance. Indirect instruction is best for advanced objectives involving analysis and process skills, good for developing student attitudes, but only moderately useful for psychomotor skills.

Thus, when an instructor is making an initial determination of what type of instruction to use, he or she could first consult this chart and, based on the objective of the instruction, make some choices about possible instructional methods. It should be noted at this point that we seldom have a single instructional objective for any session. More often we have two or three, each of which would best be served by a different instructional method. That's just fine; we encourage you to consider that mixing instructional methods within a session is a desirable strategy for a variety of reasons. Not only do different instructional methods fit different instructional objectives, but variety adds to the motivational value of a session, and different students learn better using different methods, two considerations we will address more fully later.

Let's see how this might operate in practice by considering some specific situations. For example, consider the following objectives and how different instructional methods fit their needs.

"Welcome to the library"
Objective: Students will (1) be able to list in general terms
the services offered; (2) have a positive attitude about using
the library.

This type of presentation is primarily inspirational and informational rather than instructional in the true sense of the word.
There is no great effort here to transform the students in some
major way. The purpose is to make them aware of possibilities
which they can pursue. To provide them with skills which they
will be able to use requires much more detailed instruction. So
we classify these objectives as basic cognitive and affective. We
want the students to have some basic information and to look on
the library as a possible source of help. It is not our intention to
make them avid or sophisticated library users at this point.

If we consult our chart, we see that direct instruction would
be appropriate in both cases. The direct instruction methods available to us are such things as lecture, films, tapes, demonstrations,
and printed material. Because this is basic information and because
we have affective objectives as well as cognitive objectives, we
would want the method we choose to be as simple and as interesting as possible. Therefore, we would not choose a lecturer who
might be boring. If we're going to use a lecturer, we would want to
choose someone as entertaining as possible. We would not try to
flood the students with information, but rather give them an easy
overview without too many details. Details can be provided in
written handout material. A high quality film or videotape might
serve as well, except for the affective objective. The personal presence of an engaging individual might be needed to associate the
somewhat impersonal nature of the media presentation with the
real, live close-to-home library as represented by the librarian.
Printed material would also be very effective in this situation.

"How to use the library for research"
Objective: Students will be able to use the reference materials in the library to locate information on topics of their choice.

While this is, in fact, an intermediate objective, that is, the ability to use a process, it actually consists of several sub-objectives. For example, there are some basic cognitive objectives on the types of tools available, an intermediate objective on the ability to use each of the specific tools, and possibly an affective component on the willingness to use the tools. Therefore, we might want to begin with an activity that addresses the affective component, perhaps a brief, inspirational lecture on the possibilities for time-saving through the use of search strategies, followed by another short lecture laying out the basic information about types of tools available. Then, since the next objective is an intermediate objective, we would switch to a semi-direct strategy, such as a demonstration/performance on each tool or some team-effectiveness units in which students had to work in groups to look at several paper topics using the search tools just described.

"Not all reference sources are created equal."
Objective: Students will be able to select reference sources appropriate for the question being asked.

Unlike the previous scenario, the students in this case are learning that reference sources vary in their usefulness for various types of questions. This is an advanced cognitive objective and would probably only be taught after the students already have some familiarity with the reference sources in question. The purpose here is to sharpen their skills in recognizing *appropriate* uses of the sources. Since we have an advanced cognitive objective, we would do best if we chose an indirect method, such as simulation.

In this situation, we might divide the students into small groups and give them a question and a set of sources with the instructions that the group which answers the question using the most efficient set of sources is the winner. The sources with which they would be provided would vary in their usefulness and accessibility of data. Once students had grappled with the task, the librarian would lead a discussion on the reasons for the choices made and finally summarize by pulling together what the students raised in the discussion.

The Students

From the above examples, we can see that the objective of the instruction is an important determiner of what type of instruction would be useful, but it is not the only determiner. We saw in our last example that basic familiarity with the reference sources was necessary in order to use a simulation. That brings us to our next consideration for choosing a method: the students.

One of the first characteristics of the students which one must consider in choosing an instructional method is their background in the content. Students who are beginners in a content area need to have instructional methods which are more direct, while students with a broad background can function equally well in a more unstructured environment. It is helpful to understand why this is so from the standpoint of learning. We will spend a lot more time on this premise in the chapter on learning theory, but a brief excursion at this point will help clarify the role of student background in instruction selection.

In the learning process, one of the requirements is to organize the information inputted in such a way that it can be stored easily and retrieved at a later date. Someone already very familiar with an area has a storage system in place, ready to accept new information. A student new to an area must not only take in the relevant information, but also sort out what is important and organize it. For most students, this is a difficult combination. Therefore, any instructional method which accomplishes part of the task for them will facilitate their learning.

Direct instructional systems have organization of the material as a part of their structure; thus they provide this for the students rather than ask the students to provide their own organization. It follows, therefore, that with students who are new to a content area, direct instructional methods are more useful than indirect methods. If the instructor takes great pains in a semi-direct or indirect setting to provide organization and structure, students with no background in a content can still benefit from the instruction; it simply takes longer and is less efficient.

As students become more proficient in an area and have more background information about a topic, they are capable of dealing with it even in the absence of direct instruction. They can fall back on their existing understanding of the area to provide structure and organization to new material. Therefore, with students who have some background in the content, the semi-direct and indirect methods become more reasonable.

A second student characteristic that interacts with background in the selection of instructional method is level of sophistication in learning itself. By this we mean that some students have skills in the area of learning to learn, of functioning in a nondirective environment, while others are not self-directed enough to function well in an unstructured environment. Indirect instructional methods place great demands on the students, in terms of willingness to tolerate ambiguity and to monitor and actively pursue their own learning. Direct methods require fewer new skills;

most students have had a great deal of experience learning in a direct setting. While their learning strategies may not be optimal, they will at least be familiar enough with the teaching method so that this will not distract them from the content.

The skills needed to learn in a semi-direct or indirect situation are more sophisticated and less well-practiced by most learners. Learners placed in these settings must be able to adapt their behavior to the demands of the situation. This takes not only a more sophisticated learner, but a more confident learner as well, since semi-direct and indirect methods require active responding from the student. Therefore, instructors working with graduate students can place more responsibility for the learning with the students than someone working with high schoolers.

These two characteristics also interact to color how one chooses an instructional strategy. For example, it is very possible that one would have very sophisticated learners with very little background in a particular area, and unlikely, though not impossible, to find an unsophisticated learner with a strong background in a particular content. In the former situation, precedence should be given to the background variable, but provisions made to accommodate the sophistication of the learners. For example, any direct instruction designed to provide a common background could be a lot more sophisticated in its format, pace, vocabulary, and so on, than that designed for less sophisticated learners.

The second area of Figure 4.1 compares the probable usefulness of the various instructional methods given learner characteristics. The chart indicates that direct methods are best used with learners who have little background or those without sophisticated learning skills. Semi-direct methods seem most suited to learners with medium background and/or learning skills. Indirect methods work for learners who already have a lot of background in the content or who are sophisticated learners. While none of these assessments is hard and fast with no exceptions, they should serve as a rule of thumb in selecting a method.

The Situation

The third constraint on your choice of instructional method is the one with which we are the most familiar: the situational constraint. It is probably the single most often cited reason for not trying anything unusual in the classroom. Situational constraints include such things as time allotted for instruction, number of students, classroom conditions, and availability of resources. We have placed this constraint third in line because we hope that you will not allow the situation to determine the choice of instruction, but will rather try to modify the situation to match the choice of instruction you would prefer to use. So, for example, if you are only given fifty minutes to teach the students everything they should know about the library, rather than falling back on lecture automatically, you might first consider what they need to know and how to teach that, and only later modify that scheme to fit the fifty minutes allotted; or better yet, negotiate for more time or a different situation. The assessment of various methods with respect to these variables is shown in the third section of Figure 4.1.

The first aspect of the situation to concern the instructor is the time allotted for the instruction. Direct methods require very little extra time because they are tightly controlled by the instructor. Time is not usually wasted in direct instruction. Therefore, situations with low time allotments are best used in direct instruction, depending on the objectives; when lots of time is available, it is a shame to pass up the opportunity to include student participation in the class. Semi-direct instruction takes a little more time because the instructor is depending on students' responses to questions or to the practice situation. Although the instructor is in partial control of the pace of the class, there is still some time spent clarifying incorrect answers and providing feedback to correct ones. Indirect instruction is the most time-consuming. Because the instructor gives up much of the control over the progress of the class, progress is much slower than in the other two situations.

The number of students being instructed also has an impact on the instructional method chosen. If the number is large, the more participatory methods of semi-direct and indirect instruction may become unmanageable, although not totally out of the question. Actually, in the case of large numbers, indirect methods are a little easier to handle than semi-direct because the students do much of their own instruction; the instructor merely circulates to keep things moving. Direct instruction can obviously be delivered to any number of students; however, with very small groups of four or five, it seems a shame to bypass the opportunity to involve the students in the instruction. Once again, the objectives will determine whether student involvement under those conditions would be desirable. It actually becomes a little awkward to try to lecture to such a small group.

A third consideration is the instructional setting in terms of classroom layout and facilities. Most direct group instruction systems work best in a traditional classroom setting with all the students facing the instructor. Such an arrangement makes it possible for the students to hear and see the instructor. Flexible classroom seating makes other types of instruction possible. While it is not *necessary* for semi-direct instruction, the ability of the students to see and hear both the instructor and one another can be of benefit. Most indirect forms of instruction work best when the classroom allows for flexible arrangements and movement. Students need to be able to work in groups, and both students and instructor need to be able to move around fairly easily. If the indirect instruction will occupy only a small time slot within a larger class period, fixed seating is not as big a handicap.

A final constraint of the situation is the availability of resources, such as media support and additional staff. For example, if you choose to show a film or slide show, will the room accommodate a screen and projector easily, and are they available? If you decide to use demonstration/performance, can you provide sufficient materials to allow each student to practice during the performance phase, or will the students need to work in groups? Can you enlist the assistance of other staff to circulate and monitor student progress in an indirect instructional setting? The underlying question is whether you have the facilities you need to support the instructional method you want, or must you modify the choice to meet the facilities available.

The Instructor

The last area in Figure 4.1 involves the constraints placed on the choice by the skills and preferences of the instructor. Each of the instructional methods we have been discussing requires different skills on the part of the instructor. Ideally, you can become facile at using a wide range of instructional skills, but you will always feel most comfortable with one or two favorites. If the situation permits, you should try to select methods that favor your strengths and preferences and downplay your weaknesses. If you can manage these choices, you will feel more comfortable in the class, and that comfort will be communicated to the students. Let's examine what skills might be important to our major categories of instruction.

In direct instruction, the primary skills are going to be those associated with organization and good public speaking. The instructor needs to be able to sort out what information is needed, how it can be organized to maximize understanding, and how it can be presented in such a way as to emphasize that organization. The instructor needs to be able to convey self-confidence and enthusiasm so that he or she can put the students at ease and pave the way for attention to the content. Live presenters should also be fairly skilled at "reading" an audience to determine when they are understanding the content. When a live presenter is not involved, the organization and clarity of presentation become even more important. The instructor preparing canned material needs to be able to anticipate the needs and questions of the listeners so that material covering those questions and needs can be included in the presentation.

Instructor skills in semi-direct instruction take two forms. There is a need for presentation skills in demonstration/performance teaching so that the initial information can be conveyed effectively; there is also the need to monitor student performance during the performance phase, being able to identify problems and provide guidance and feedback both to individuals and the group as a whole. In case-study classes or reviews, the instructor skills are those of asking questions and giving feedback. Instructors who select this type of teaching should also have patience, since they will have to monitor student progress directly and students don't always do what you expect them to. The instructor needs to be able to follow the students' lead without constant intervention if the students are to learn to perform some of the complex problem solving that this type of instruction often aims at.

Of the three types of instruction we are discussing, the one requiring the greatest range of instructor skills is oddly enough the one where the instructor's role is the least obvious: the indirect instructional system. To be able to teach using indirect methods, an instructor must be able to construct exercises that make sense to the learners and provide good instructions so that the instructor's direct intervention will not be needed very often. The instructor must have a great deal of self-control in order not to intervene while the students are working. He or she must have good listening skills and summarizing/consolidating skills in order to conduct the debriefing and base it on the experiences of the students. The instructor must be flexible enough to handle any outcome of the instruction which might surface, since one of the hallmarks of indirect instruction is variety.

Thus we can see from the above descriptions that different instructor qualities are appropriate for different instructional systems. If you are not currently skilled at a particular type of instruction, we encourage you to try it anyway, but to do so within a setting and with material you already know well. It is not a good idea to try to develop new teaching skills and new materials at the same time. Once you become skilled at all types of instruction, you can use your preferences for one type or another to help you choose among the alternatives, provided you have taken the other three constraints into consideration.

SEQUENCING THE INSTRUCTION

We stated earlier that it is rare for one instructional method to be appropriate for all situations and that we encourage you to incorporate variety into the instructional setting. Another useful way to think about incorporating variety involves the sequencing of instruction. What activity should come when?

Svinicki and Dixon (1987) have proposed a system for selecting and sequencing instruction which builds on Kolb's Experiential

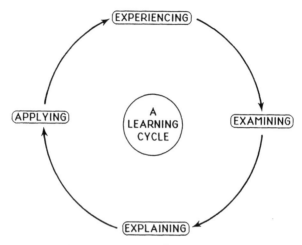

Figure 4.2 A modification of Kolb's Learning Cycle.

Learning Cycle (1984) and is fairly easy for the beginning instructor to follow. In this system, learning is conceived of as involving four points on a circle, as shown in Figure 4.2. Learning begins with a concrete *experience* with the environment. The learner then *examines* that experience and tries to make some sense of it. This reflection process results in a tentative *explanation* for the experience, which is a combination of previous experiences, ideas, and new concepts. The learner then *applies* this explanation in preparing for the next encounter with a similar situation. On the basis of that plan, more experience occurs which cycles around to refine the explanation, and the learner learns more and more from the experience.

If this cycle does indeed describe how the learner adapts to the new environment, then it seems logical that an instructor could follow this path in the sequencing of instruction and take advantage of the natural learning sequence. This is precisely what Svinicki and Dixon propose. In sequencing instruction, they suggest that instructors begin with a concrete experience of some sort and then let the students examine that experience as they try to build an explanation for it. Once an explanation or model is constructed to describe the experience, the students test out that explanation on a new instance of the phenomenon to see if the explanation is accurate. If they are able to apply the new concept, then they have learned; if they are not able to apply it, more examination and further attempts to explain are needed.

Let's look at an example. If we wanted to help students understand how different indexes draw on different kinds of information sources, we might begin with a concrete experience in which we give each student in a group a different index and ask each to scan through the index and produce a list of the journals cited in that index. Then we would have the group work together to compare their lists and try to find some sort of regularities in the types of journals cited, an activity that would encourage them to examine this information more closely. Then as a large group, we could ask students to describe any regularities they found. This would be followed by a mini-lecture explaining the differences between the types of sources they found and how that information would be useful to them. We could have the group identify which types of journals are found in which indexes and discuss the type of information which would be available in them. Finally, we could have the students apply this new schema for locating information by giving them topics to locate and having them make predictions about which index would be likely to have that kind of information.

In the above example, which is illustrated in Figure 4.3, we have taken the students completely around the cycle. Our objective was that they would be able to identify which indexes would be useful for particular topics. This is a fairly complex objective. To achieve it, we are using mostly group work involving discussion

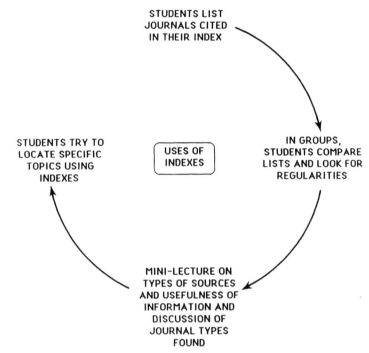

Figure 4.3   An instructional sequence beginning with experiencing.

and simulation, where the students' skills would be able to handle the ambiguities of the task. In the middle, where we do have a basic information-transfer task, we have used a mini-lecture; however, we are soon back to a simulation, asking the students to apply what they have discovered to some new information.

Another example of using the cycle to sequence instruction is illustrated in Figure 4.4. Here we might be teaching students how to narrow a topic for purposes of doing a computer search. We might begin with an activity in which we ask the students to suggest a topic on which we might want to do a search. They are likely to suggest something fairly broad initially (the same inference can be made for topic widening as well). This suggestion

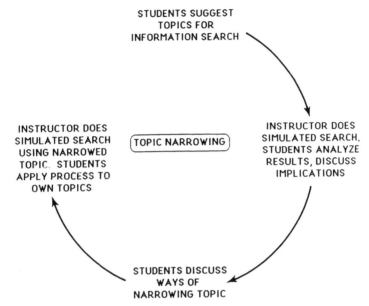

Figure 4.4   An instructional sequence beginning with experiencing.

could then be looked up to see just how many references there might be on that topic. This step could be repeated for several suggested topics. The students might then be asked to discuss the consequences of having so many references and why the topic they suggested might have produced such a large number. Then the group could be asked to generate ways of reducing the number of references. They would probably make suggestions that would fit into the topic narrowing model. The librarian could then determine how the newly narrowed topics would fare in terms of references produced. If more narrowing is needed, the process could be repeated. Or the librarian could then demonstrate one of the processes commonly used for topic narrowing and show how it would affect the number of references available. Finally, the students could be asked to apply the topic narrowing procedures to their own topics.

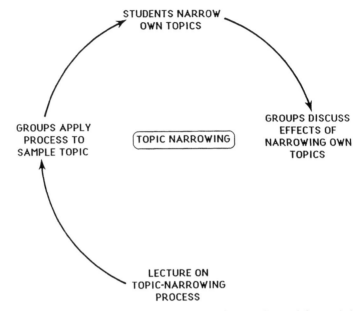

Figure 4.5 An instructional sequence beginning with explaining.

The original experiential learning cycle began consistently at the concrete experience point, but Svinicki and Dixon feel that an argument can be made for starting at the explaining point in many cases. In this situation, the instruction begins with the explanation of how things are supposed to work, followed by an attempt on the part of students to apply what has just been explained. That experience then is examined to see how well the students' experiences matched the ideal. For example, the librarian might begin with an explanation of the topic-narrowing procedure and then have the students apply it to a sample topic. Then they attempt to narrow their own topics, followed by a discussion of how well they were able to accomplish the narrowing. This sequence is illustrated in Figure 4.5.

Choosing one starting point over the other depends on both the sophistication of the learners and their motivation level. If they are fairly sophisticated, it would probably be better from a learning point of view to begin with the concrete experience and let the learners discover the principles for themselves. Also if they need some motivation, the concrete experience starting point is preferable since it has a built-in motivation, since they see the consequences of their experiences. On the other hand, with limited time or unsophisticated learners, it might be better to start with the explanation point of the cycle to make things go more smoothly.

One can also see that a logical extension of this theory is the idea that certain instructional activities promote certain types of learning activities around the cycle. For example, in order to give the learners concrete experience, the instructor must use hands-on demonstration/performance or simulations. To give the learners a chance to examine their experiences, the instructor needs some discussion or group work or perhaps journals or diaries outside of class. Explanation generation can be done in a lecture, or the group can do it in a discussion which is directed by the instructor. The application step requires practice activities, simulations, case studies, or anything in which the student is applying what has been learned to a new situation.

The cycles described above seem to combine direct, semi-direct, and indirect instructional methods in fairly systematic ways. Cycles starting at the experience point of the circle begin with indirect methods in the experiencing and examining phases, move to direct instruction in the explaining phase, and on to semi-direct or indirect in the application phase. Cycles beginning with explaining use direct instruction in that phase, semi-direct in the application phase and experience phase, and indirect in the examining phase. On the basis of this sequencing, one might conclude that in order to begin with concrete experience, you would need learners who were fairly sophisticated either in background or in learning. The second of these two is probably more important since we are trying to get the learners to extract information from these experiences. Novice learners need the structure of direct methods initially and would probably best begin at the explanation phase. There is one additional consideration, however: The motivation level of the learners may play a role here. If students are fairly unconvinced of the usefulness of this instruction, the experiences they have in some of those indirect methods should have a good motivating effect on them.

Svinicki and Dixon also suggest that there can be degrees of direct involvement of the students with an activity, similar to the continuum of instructor-directed versus student-directed learning discussed earlier. It is possible during the course of a lecture for an instructor to elicit many of the same reactions from the students that he or she would get if they were personally experiencing something. For instance, the use of examples prior to giving an explanation is similar to giving the students experiences on which to reflect. The rhetorical question causes the students to stop and think or examine what is being said more closely. Obviously, an instructor can incorporate an explanation into a lecture and can use more examples to show how the explanation applies in real situations. Just as with our discussion of direct instruction, we would suggest that the more the students are actively involved in the learning, the better it will be; however, we recognize that learner, situation, and instructor constraints often restrict the number of choices you have.

IN SUMMARY

We have now seen that the set of instructional activities you choose will be determined by what you are trying to accomplish, who is in your audience, what the instructional conditions are, and who you are. In addition, using a natural learning sequence to guide your choice of activities will help you incorporate more variety into the instructional sessions you design.

REFERENCES

Bloom, B. S. (Ed.). (1956). *A Taxonomy of Educational Objectives, Handbook I: The Cognitive Domain*, David McKay Company, New York.

Kolb, D. A. (1984). *Experiential Learning: Experience as the Source of Learning and Development*, Prentice-Hall, Englewood Cliffs, New Jersey.

Svinicki, M. D., and Dixon, N. M. (1987). "The Kolb Model Modified for Classroom Activities." *College Teaching, 35* (4), pp. 141-146.

5
Learning Theory Applied to Instruction

Even when the instructor goes to great lengths to select a unit of learning activities that fit the goals, students, and environment, and to sequence these activities effectively, there are things that can be done to enhance the learning environment even further. The purpose of this chapter is to provide you with a practical set of guidelines based on a distillation of learning theory from a variety of sources. If, in the design and conduct of your instruction, you try to incorporate these four principles, you have a good chance of achieving a respectable amount of learning by the students.

FOUR BASIC PRINCIPLES FOR LEARNING

The distilled theory resolves itself into four areas for intervention, represented by the acronym MORF. These letters stand for the following:

Motivation
Organization
Response
Feedback

This acronym thus becomes the key to remembering these four areas. They are based on our ideas about the critical variables in learning and where an instructor can intervene in the process.

The learning structure is shown in Figure 5.1. It begins with a learner who needs to be *motivated*, either internally or externally, to engage in the learning process. This step presents the first opportunity for the instructor to intervene. It corresponds roughly to the "experiencing" step in our earlier cycle, since much motivation to start learning comes from our experience with the environment.

The next step in the process involves *organizing* the content to be learned so that it can be stored in permanent memory. This step, which corresponds to "examining" and "explaining" in our previous model, provides the second opportunity for the instructor to intervene. Organization has two parts: Once the student is motivated to begin the process, he or she must identify the material to be learned from an often vast amount of information which is presented (examining); once the relevant material has been identified, it resides in short-term memory while the learner tries to organize it or understand its existing organization (explaining).

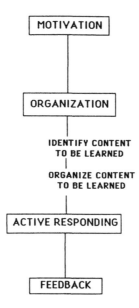

Figure 5.1   Points for intervention in learning.

In the process of organizing the information for permanent storage in long-term memory, the learner needs to be actively engaged with the content, making some individual *response* to the material (applying), a third opportunity for the instructor to intervene by structuring the opportunities for responding. Once the response has occurred, the learner needs to receive *feedback* on his or her understanding of the content (also part of applying), which is the fourth point of intervention for the instructor. If the feedback is positive, indicating that the learner has correctly understood and applied the content, he or she can move on to the next material to be learned. If the feedback indicates that the student did not understand the content, instruction should return to the earlier step of content identification and organization to determine where in the process the learner became confused. This process repeats itself until the learner responds correctly.

This simple version of the learning cycle now becomes a useful tool for instructional design because it has implications for what the instructor needs to include in the instructional sequence. The rest of this chapter describes each of these points in more detail and provides suggestions on their implications for instructional activities. At the end of the chapter, we will examine each of our instructional methods to see how they incorporate these four principles in their structure.

Motivation

The first principle of learning that applies to designing instruction is motivation. Although it sometimes seems learning can occur in the absence of motivation for many of us who have been subjected to a lot of boring courses, it is far more efficient in a motivated learner. Below is a list of the most commonly mentioned motivators for learning.

Common Motivators

Need to Know. One strong motivator for learning a new skill or set of information is a need for the information in order to complete some other task or do some other job. For example, teaching students to use reference materials is particularly difficult unless they have a paper to do that requires them to review the literature. That is why an important intervention for a librarian is to tie the instruction into course assignments which the students must complete. The librarian should consider both the timing of the presentation of material and the content which is presented. Too many course instructors schedule library instruction when it is convenient for them, rather than at a time when the information is needed by the students. The librarian should work with the course instructor to identify a time or times when the students would be most receptive to the content. Likewise, the librarian should work with the course instructor to identify the skills the students will need and limit the instruction to those skills, rather than trying to tell them everything they need to know about information gathering.

Curiosity. Another strong motivator for learning is the unanswered question, the novel experience, the unexpected result. Learners confronted with a puzzle will usually try to solve it; therefore, an instructor can often capitalize on this tendency by beginning presentations with questions, paradoxes, or simple problems to stimulate curiosity. For example, in a session on where to find various types of information, the librarian could begin the class with a modified version of "Trivial Pursuit," first having each individual student try to match each bit of information with the source from which it comes and then having them work in groups to pool their answers. The succeeding lecture on the various information sources would use the game as the basis for its organization. One could even award a prize to the individual and the group getting the most answers correct.

Relevance. Demonstrating the relevance of new information or skills to other aspects of the students' existence will also serve as a source of motivation. This can be done by slanting the presentation to the content interests of the students or by using those interest areas as the settings for analogies and examples of new material. For example, in a session designed to teach topic narrowing to a history class, you obviously would use history topics. Alternatively, using topics of general interest to the students is equally effective; for instance, using examples of current events, especially those on campus, often stimulates student interest. You could use a topic like "undergraduate education" as a broad topic needing narrowing. Building on this last point, we would also suggest making yourself familiar with the everyday concerns of your potential audience pool so that you can tie your content to those concerns. For example, many students think they don't organize their time efficiently; emphasizing how some of the research techniques you will be suggesting helps in that area could capture their attention.

Success. The sources of motivation listed above apply mostly to getting the learning started. It is just as important to keep the learning going once it starts, and nothing succeeds like success. The instructor who incorporates activities which are readily accomplished without being mindless is taking advantage of the motivating properties of success itself. For example, in the case cited above about using a game to stimulate curiosity, some of the items should be straightforward enough to allow the students to experience some success in answering the questions. If they cannot answer any of the questions, they will lose interest because they are experiencing only failure. A sprinkling of correct answers gives the students a feeling of control and empowers them to learn.

Interest Value of Material. This motivator may seem fairly obvious, yet it's surprising how often we forget to consider it when selecting materials and methods for instruction. There are many different ways of presenting the same information. Some serve to motivate the learner because they are inherently well done and interesting; others tend to stifle motivation. Material that contains a lot of variety and examples is inherently more interesting, regardless of the topic, than material that is monotonous or very abstract. One can easily see this point in the formats of various scientific journals versus something like *Scientific American*. The content of articles in the latter is no less scholarly or complex than those in more professional journals, but the format and presentation of *Scientific American* articles are far more interesting and, therefore, inherently more motivating. Perhaps we should keep in our mind's eye the model of *Scientific American* when thinking about designing inherently interesting presentations.

A Lively Model.   One source of motivation we often are unaware of is the influence of the model the instructor provides of an enthusiastic learner. It is hard for students to get excited about online searching if you yourself can't work up any enthusiasm about it. A lively, energetic instructor goes a long way toward motivating students to pay attention and give the material a fair shake.

What Does All This Mean for Instruction?

We have already given several specific examples of how a librarian can incorporate the principle of motivation into the instructional design. Now we'd like to give a broader view of the principle itself and how it can be used.

The underlying message in all the examples above is that the librarian cannot take the motivation level of the students for granted. Rather, the librarian must make a conscious effort to incorporate some form of motivation into the instructional design, directly or indirectly. Indirect methods include timing the instruction to maximize the students' need for it, incorporating challenging and novel experiences into the instruction, and attempting to make the presentation as varied and inherently interesting as possible. More direct methods involve making the material as relevant to the concerns of the learners as possible and incorporating successful experiences with the material into the instruction.

It should be noted that we are advocating the use of positive forms of motivation, rather than negative motivators such as threats or fear of failure. There are several reasons for this preference. In the first place, few librarians have the authority in a class that would allow them to be effective in the use of negative control. More important, however, are the relative long-term effects of positive versus negative motivation. While negative forms of motivation have more immediate effects on the learner, they also have many undersirable side effects. Positive motivators are less powerful, but have desirable side effects of long-term goodwill and positive affect toward the resources available in the library. We mention this only to make the point that in addition to the cognitive objectives you are most likely to be emphasizing, you will also have attitudinal objectives about library use and confidence in librarians. The more you can associate positive experiences with library instruction and librarians, the more sucessful you will be in achieving those objectives.

The timing of these motivators is also important. The instructor should make an effort to have something of a motivational character at the very outset of the instructional sequence in order to get the attention of the learners. This attention-getter should be followed by conscious attempts to keep the learners involved throughout the instruction by incorporating a variety of presentation methods and activities as described in chapters 3 and 4.

Organization

Once motivated, the learner must begin the actual learning itself. One way to conceive of learning is the storage of information and skills in long-term memory so that they can be easily retrieved and used at a future time, just as we store books in the library for easy access. In our original discussion of the learning process, we said that this phase of the learning has two parts: first, identifying what is to be learned, similar to determining the major characteristics of a book before it receives its Library of Congress call number, and second, organizing what is to be learned so that it can be stored and retrieved, similar to setting up a classification system like the LC system. Let's look at these steps in turn.

Identifying Information To Be Learned
We are constantly being bombarded by stimulation from the environment. Some of it is important, but most of it is not. Therefore, even though we do "receive" these stimulus inputs, we do

not necessarily respond to them "consciously," unless we have a reason to or they are brought to our attention somehow. There are lots of examples of this in everyday life. We are not normally aware of our rate of breathing until someone brings it to our attention or it varies significantly from the normal. The same is true for auditory stimulation. Most of the time we do not "hear" ninety percent of the sounds around us, but if someone asks, "What's that noise?" we immediately become aware of it. Likewise, there are some sounds that will get a person's attention immediately, whether or not anyone else has called attention to them. For example, a mother of small children will respond immediately when there is a change in the sounds from her child, even if the child is not in the same room or the change is from noise to quiet. We see a similar situation in visual stimulation. Until we have a reason to notice something, most of us can give only the vaguest description of objects in our environment. However, if there is a reason to notice something, such as a landmark along our daily journey to work, those objects can be described, while everything else around them is reported as a blur.

Another characteristic of attention and storage is that if the learner cannot differentiate what is important for later recall, he or she will end up storing *all* the information (or as much as possible) in a haphazard manner, making it very difficult to sort out later. Occasionally, this can lead to the phenomenon of information overload, in which the attempt to store everything results in the retention of nothing.

What Does This Imply for Instruction?   These very well-documented phenomena translate directly into instructional practice. If we want a learner to learn some information, we must first make it stand out from its environment. Our students will do this themselves as they try to study the content of a course. They highlight sentences in the textbook, take notes in class, and so on. These activities are designed to make certain information stand out from the rest so it will will be learned. Unfortunately, many times the things they choose to highlight are not the things we would like them to learn. They often "miss the point" and attend to things that more readily fit into their own "highlighting" method. It's easy to recognize facts and figures; it's more difficult to highlight an underlying principle which is being developed over the course of an hour's lecture.

We as instructors, therefore, must be aware of what the important information is and strive to make that information stand out from all the details and elaborations used to clarify the information. Textbooks do this all the time by varying the type they use. Bold type, italics, underlining, and so on are all techniques used to make major points stand out from the rest. Instructors can do something similar by learning to "speak in italics or bold type," that is, use their voices to emphasize critical information. "Dramatic" pauses before and after main points, changes in inflection, and changes in tone are all ways that an instructor signals the importance of the information.

Props, primarily visual aids, also facilitate directing attention. A change in the visual environment will momentarily focus attention on the new source of information. At that time, a critical point can be made and is more likely to be noticed.

Verbal cues can also be used to make information stand out from the background. It may sound corny, but saying something like "this is an important point" or repeating verbatim a critical point cues the students' attention effectively.

The students can also be primed before the learning activity to notice critical information when it surfaces. This is done by providing the students with an outline, a pretest, a set of questions, or a set of objectives at the beginning of the activity. These items produce an attention "set" in the student so that when information relevant to any of those items shows up later, it tends to attract attention.

The important point for the instructor to remember is that he or she must highlight what is to be learned and make the important information and concepts stand out from the background explanatory material. Until the learners know what they should be learning, they will have a hard time learning what we intend, even though they are probably learning something.

Classifying the Information To Be Learned
The second step in learning information or skills is to organize and classify the information so that it can be entered into our memory system and stored. Of course, no one knows for sure what a human memory system looks like or how it works, but there are some reasonable hypotheses which seem to fit with the data and certainly can be used as a model for thinking about learning and memory. First of all, there seem to be levels of memory: from transient impressions, which fade quickly, to short-term memory, a sort of immediate work area containing the information we're dealing with right at the moment, to long-term memory, which is like the Smithsonian of the system, storing all the information we have acquired over the years, more or less available to be called up for use in current activities. Hopefully our students eventually put the contents of the courses into long-term memory and in such a way that those memories can be readily retrieved.

What is long-term memory storage like? Of course, we have only models, but one which is useful in instructional design is that of an immense cross-referenced network. For each concept or memory there is a central category. Attached to that core are relevant attributes which can also serve as categories. They are attached to each other in varying degrees of strength, depending on their prominence. The system can be entered at any point, and the probability of eliciting the other nodes in the system depends on how strongly they are connected. So, for example, in one memory system, the central concept "dog" might have as one of its subcategories "animal" and, further off, "mammal," although the latter is not a strong association unless you're in biology. A stronger association could be "pet" and, possibly through that link, "cat." Other attributes attached to the "dog" concept would depend on our experiences with dogs in the real world. We might have a particular dog in mind, one that we had as a pet, or unpleasant past experiences might associate "dog" with "things to be avoided."

The entire network would be very complex, but people with similar backgrounds and similar cultures would have similar major categories and associations. New information entering the system is first classified according to its most prominent attributes (which often depend on the situation in which it is encountered), and this mini-network is overlaid on the existing network, where similar categories form connections. The more often the new information is encountered, the stronger those bonds become and the more other bonds are developed, since the situations in which the information is encountered cannot possibly be identical.

What Does This Imply for Instruction?   What we want to do as teachers is to facilitate the correct and efficient categorization of information and then provide plenty of repetition and opportunities for the information to be recalled and restored in memory, so that it can be easily retrieved in the future when we're not around. We can start by providing an organizational system. Information presented in a well-organized manner has a much higher probability of being stored according to that system than information haphazardly presented. Therefore, instructors should put a lot of time into developing an overall scheme for organizing the information in their discipline. One caution to this idea, however, is that if the instructional goal is to teach the students to provide their own organizational systems for unorganized information, the instructor shouldn't do it for them.

Another helpful procedure is to look for organization schema that the students already use or understand and use those as the basis for presenting new information which is organized along similar lines. This is the rationale for the use of analogies as teaching aids. The analogy calls out of memory a particular set of connections and organizational structures. By comparing the new information to that pre-existing structure, the student can more readily classify and organize the new information. For example, a librarian trying to explain how a thesaurus is used might compare it to a diet-exchange system, in which you need one portion of meat (a major heading), which could be steak or hamburger or stew meat (narrower terms) or fish (related term), and so on. Sometimes this can backfire on an instructor if the system being used as an analogy is not one the students understand anyway. It doesn't do any good to use an explanation that no one can understand to explain a concept that no one can understand. For this reason, instructors are encouraged to draw on the things with which the students are familiar or find interesting already. Examples operate in much the same way, though less directly.

For the instructor, the primary message of this principle of learning is that information to be learned needs to be given structure, either by the learner or the instructor, in order to be stored efficiently and used at a later date. Therefore, in designing an instructional sequence, the instructor must first have a clear conceptualization of the content to be learned and how it all fits together.

Then the instructor must either help the learners to develop that structure themselves, through activities and discussion, or provide that structure during the learning.

Active Responding

A third area of learning theory that is pertinent to the design of instruction is the support of active responding as the best method for learning. We would never think of learning a physical skill simply by watching someone else do it, but somehow when it comes to learning information or information-processing skills, we seem to think it's sufficient to merely read or hear about the information once. Thus many instructors operate on the assumption that if the students have had a lecture on how to do library research, they will be able to do it immediately.

Quite the contrary is the case. If we want to say that something has been learned, the learner must be able to use that information or skill. Until then, we have no evidence that the information/skill has been correctly stored in memory. The incorporation of active responding into instruction provides the opportunity for a learner to test if his or her understanding of the material is accurate.

Active responding also contributes to the transfer of learning to real-world situations. The students must learn to use information in an active way: to search through the files of knowledge and ideas stored away, find those pieces which are useful to a particular problem, and apply them to the solution. Until the students are placed in the position of using the information we have given them, the only application situations in which their understanding is tested are those which they generate for themselves. These may or may not match the situations we would choose for them. For example, many students "test" themselves by reading through their lecture notes, silently nodding whenever they recognize something. This recognition is not the same response they will face on an exam or in real life. Unfortunately, our students have very few alternative systems for self-testing. The more situations we can provide in which the material or skills can be used, the more likely it is that the learning will transfer to real-life use.

Active responding also serves as a motivator for the learner. Active responding sets the stage for evidence of progress, which is one of the key motivators of learning. Without this evidence of progress, a learner may be hard pressed to maintain attention to the task and continue to take in new information.

What Does This Imply for Instruction?
Since active responding is such an important component of learning, the instructor should make an effort to incorporate opportunities for activity into instruction as often as possible. We have already discussed several alternative ways of making students active by using semi-direct and indirect teaching methods. Granted this will take time away from information presentation, but the learning of what is included will be better if active responding is a part of the instruction.

This active responding should be a part of the instruction itself. For example, we have already seen that beginning a session with an activity that engages the students' attention, such as a group contest involving questions about the session's content, can set the tone for the rest of the class. Another good starting activity is to have the students reflect on their past experiences with whatever the topic of the day is, such as what problems or successes they have experienced in using the library or where they have gone in the library to find information of a given type. Once the students have individually reflected on these experiences, the librarian can have them compare notes and look for common themes.

Hopefully these can then become the themes which the librarian can use to organize the rest of the session.

During the presentation of material, the librarian can incorporate questions for the entire class. These questions can be factual-type questions which the students are likely to know already or questions asking the students to apply a concept that has just been described to a real situation. Often you can ask for examples from individual students, especially if they have had some previous experience with the content at some level.

An important aspect of the use of questions during instruction is the provision for thinking time once the question has been asked. Too often instructors become discouraged in using questions because it seems that the students are slow in responding. It must be remembered, however, that there are several steps a student must go through in order to answer a question in class, and those steps take time. The student must first be sure of what the question was, then the question must be interpreted, then an answer must be formulated, and finally the student must muster the courage to offer that answer up for public inspection. The more complex the question, the more time needed. Yet most instructors have trouble waiting as little as three seconds before starting to fidget.

A useful technique is to frame the question in such a way as to force thinking time. For example, the librarian might say, "Take a moment and jot down for yourself a couple of examples of how computer-aided searching can save you time." Then the librarian slowly and silently counts to twenty, resisting the urge to say anything in the interim. Then when the librarian opens the floor for contributions, the students have had a chance to think and, therefore, are more likely to have something to contribute.

Another useful active-responding technique is the content-focused problem-solving discussion during class. It involves the use of exercises during the class period that get the student to use, critique, or defend the information being learned. For example, after describing a process for evaluating the usefulness of various information sources for a given question, the librarian could divide the class up into small groups or pairs, give each a list of questions, and have the groups work at selecting an appropriate source for each question.

Alternatively, the librarian might structure the entire class period as a group problem-solving task, beginning the session with the statement of the problem: "We have an assignment to write a paper on the impact of war in Central America on the American economy. What are some ways of starting this project?" The class would then suggest alternative activities in a brainstorming fashion, while the librarian writes these suggestions on the board. Then the librarian would go back over the suggestions and, with the help of the class, evaluate them and put the ones that survive the evaluation in some sequence. At that point, the librarian should confirm the sequence the class has generated by comparing it with the normally recommended sequence for doing a research paper. Then the class could be asked to identify what resources they would need at each step they have generated and where those might be found. The librarian would confirm the sources as the list is generated, adding any that the students might be unfamiliar with. The final formal part of the session would be a summary of what has been discussed to make sure that all points have been covered. The session could then be ended with an additional activity in which the individual students spend some time creating an action plan for their own papers, based on the process just completed with the class as a whole.

This last example of active responding was a rather elaborate one, involving a lot of responding on the part of the students, but much simpler plans would be effective as well. One variation of active responding we would recommend is the use of pairs or groups to work on more complex problems. Students can learn a great deal from one another in group problem-solving tasks, and the group effort increases the probability that the students will get the correct answer. The group also serves as moral support for students who are less sure of their own abilities and thus encourages more students to become actively involved. On simpler tasks, however, individual work is appropriate because of the time factor. The important thing to remember is that the incorporation of active responding into the instruction will greatly benefit the learning process.

Feedback

The final step in the learning sequence is the delivery of feedback to the learner after a response. One reason for including active responding in learning is to give the learner some idea of how well his or her internal system for processing new information functions when faced with a real question. The capstone on the process is the feedback itself. The learner *will* receive feedback whenever he or she responds. The question then becomes who controls that feedback and how well does it advance our goals of teaching the student.

To make this point clearer, let's consider an example. Have you ever listened to individuals singing along with the radio while wearing headphones which block out their own voices? The amount of feedback they are receiving on the accuracy of pitch and loudness is minimal. It is coming primarily from the sensations produced by the muscles in the throat and diaphragm, not a particularly good source, but a source nevertheless. Now take their headphones off and let them hear themselves. Their performances improve immediately because the feedback is now directed at pitch and loudness. The same is true for learning. Appropriate feedback greatly enhances performance.

What Does This Imply for Instruction?

The feedback a learner receives can come from many sources. It can be given directly by the instructor, which is desirable because it can then be tailored to the individual's needs. It is also almost guaranteed to be more accurate. However, it is a rare situation that allows the librarian to devote as much time to individual feedback as is desirable. Therefore, the librarian would be well advised to set up the *learning environment* to provide feedback and then teach the students how to recognize and benefit from it. Models, such as examples of completed work and demonstrations followed by active practice experiences, provide sources of feedback for the students against which they can compare their own efforts. Therefore, if the session is about reference sources, the librarian should provide printed examples of good bibliographies, with an explanation of why various sources were included. Or if an exercise is used to see how well the students can order the steps in a search sequence, there should be a written feedback sheet which lists the steps and the reasons for their order. In each case, the student could go back over his or her own responses and compare them with the model, identifying where there were differences and why.

Another possible source of feedback is the other students, with periodic monitoring from the librarian. For example, once the group has gone over the process of how to narrow a paper topic and tried it as a group with a sample topic, individual students can attempt the process with their paper topics. After a few moments, pairs of students can examine each other's work and determine how the author came to the final topic. The other member

of the pair can ask questions and help evaluate the application of
the procedure to the given topic.

Although a librarian rarely has extensive exposure to a given
class, we want to note that an instructor can also allow students to
critique their own behavior while the instructor evaluates the critiques. For example, if you were working with a class over a pro-
longed period, you could have them keep a journal about the steps
they took to research a given issue and then write a description
and evaluation of those steps from the standpoint of good search
technique. Their ability to describe why they made certain decisions and where they went wrong or right would become the basis
for evaluating their progress. The advantage to such a procedure is
that as the students become skillful in self-analysis, the need for
direct instructor feedback decreases. The students become self-
directed learners, which is what they need to do if they are to survive on their own.

LEARNING PRINCIPLES AND INSTRUCTIONAL TYPES

As you might have concluded by now, the different instructional
types which we discussed earlier differ in the degree to which they
incorporate these four principles of learning. Because of this, the
instructor should be aware of their strengths and weaknesses in
this regard, in order to compensate for them. The purpose of this
section is to evaluate the instructional types and their attention to
these learning principles, as illustrated in Figure 5.2, and to suggest
ways in which the instructor can minimize the impact of the deficits.

Direct Instruction

Motivation
Most forms of direct instruction are not inherently motivating. In
fact, most lectures can be pretty dry and uninteresting. On the

	M	O	R	F
DIRECT	varies; requires intervention	very good	very poor	very poor
SEMI-DIRECT	fairly good	fairly good	very good	very good
INDIRECT	very good	very poor; requires intervention	very good	possible but delayed; must be monitored

Figure 5.2 Evaluation of instructional methods by learning principles.

other hand, a really well-organized and presented lecture on a relevant topic can be a motivating experience. But it is safe to say that of the three instructional types, direct instruction requires the most active intervention on the part of the instructor if it is to motivate the students to learn.

The instructor must pay attention to most of those methods of motivation discussed earlier and incorporate them into the direct instruction. For example, the topic must be relevant, and that relevance must be made clear to the learners. It is a good idea to start direct instruction with something to stimulate the curiosity of the learners: a question, a puzzle, a common experience with which they can identify. During the instruction, it is useful to incorporate questions, even if they must be rhetorical questions, because not only do they engage the students' minds as they try to answer the questions, but they set the stage for successful experiences if the students can guess at the answers to the questions. Feelings of success are also generated if the presentation is clear and easy to follow. As long as the students believe they are understanding what is being offered, they will feel good about their own abilities and kindly toward the person doing the instruction.

Perhaps the most important and most controllable is the presentation mode itself. Direct presentations need variety and stimulation incorporated into their very structure. If the direct instruction is a lecture, the lecturer must be enthusiastic and lively. If the direct instruction is a film, it should be well paced and colorful. If the direct instruction is printed material, it should be attractive and eye catching. Many instructors object to this as "flash" rather than substance, but we must keep in mind that in order to teach anything, we have to keep the learners' attention, and we are usually dealing with a far more sophisticated audience in terms of exposure to attractively designed presentations than used to be the case. Only our best effort can compete with that history.

Organization

Of all the four learning principles, this is the one where direct presentation methods really shine. Because the instructor is in control of the instruction constantly when using direct instruction methods, he or she is able to maintain a good organization and flow of information. In fact, one of the first things an instructor does to prepare for a direct presentation is to "organize" the information. Therefore, it is a rare direct presentation that is not organized conceptually, at least as far as the instructor is concerned.

However, that does not necessarily mean that the learners will see it as organized. The instructor must make an active effort to be sure that the internal organization on which the presentation is based is clear to the learners. As we discussed in the section on organization, the instructor must use cuing and other devices to insure that the students are paying attention at those times when important information is being offered. The instructor should make the organization of the presentation explicit by providing an outline of what will be included from the very start. The outline need not be extensive, but the inclusion of major headings will help the students see where the presentation is going and provide benchmarks of progress as the presentation proceeds. Then, as the presentation unfolds, the instructor should refer to the outline to keep the students aware of their progress.

One final aspect of organization which is often a problem with direct presentations is the tendency to include too much information in a single sitting. While it is true that the better the organization the more that can be included, it is still a good idea not to overwhelm the students with details. It is best to include about one main topic for every ten minutes of instruction and keep the number of subtopics under each main topic down to two or three. Even if you have more information than that to include, if you can organize it according to a structure similar to this, you will have a better chance of getting some learning than if you don't.

Active Responding
As you may have gathered earlier, one of the hallmarks of direct instruction is a distinct lack of active responding on the part of the learners. Therefore, this is an area where an instructor must make a special effort to identify ways of encouraging student response without actually changing the nature of the instruction.

The most obvious way of doing this is to take advantage of the natural tendency of learners to try to answer questions, even if not put to them directly. For example, in the outline described above under organization, the librarian can accomplish two ends at once by phrasing the main points of the outline in the form of questions. Therefore, rather than having the main point read "Alternative Indexes for Information on Population," the outline would read "What are some of the indexes that contain information about population?" or, more generally, "Where can we get information about population?" The question format frames the way the student will listen to the presentation under that heading into a more active, problem-solving mode.

The same effect is accomplished through the use of rhetorical questions sprinkled throughout the presentation. When some information is preceded by a question like "Why would we choose one type of index over another?" the students are put into a particular learning set of answering that question and thus are more active in their listening.

Of course, in any direct presentation session, there is a continuum of learner participation if the instructor allows questions to be asked or asks questions of the audience. This is a form of active responding. We encourage the provision of opportunities to ask and answer questions in these types of instructional situations, but we also recognize that questions are often not possible.

Feedback
Since direct instruction includes few opportunities for active responding on the part of the learners, it also offers few opportunities for feedback. In these instructional situations, the closest thing to feedback is the provision of periodic summaries. When the instruction reaches a point where a summary is appropriate, the learners can compare their understanding of what has just been covered with the summary provided by the instructor. If the two match, then the learners' understanding is confirmed and the feedback is positive. If they differ, the learners realize that they have missed something and need to ask for clarification or to pursue other avenues of finding the information missed. Therefore, it would be wise to make periodic summaries of the concepts presented and how they fit together, to allow the learners to critique their own understanding of the material.

Semi-Direct Instruction

Motivation

The primary source of motivation in semi-direct instruction lies in the objectives. This type of instruction has very practical, task-oriented, problem-solving objectives. Students are learning to do something, to apply some rules, to accomplish some task, and therefore, the need to carry out the task becomes the motivation for engaging in the learning.

This does not absolve the instructor from a responsibility for monitoring the motivation of the students. For one thing, the students may not realize why they need to learn this particular procedure or skill. It may be up to the instructor to make the connection between what students are learning to do and the "big picture" of the course or their academic careers or whatever.

Also, the instructor is responsible for seeing that the students will have successful experiences when they get to the actual application of the learning. Care must be taken to move slowly enough through the process and allow the students to try one part of the task at a time so they will be successful and, therefore, wish to continue. Nothing will kill student motivation faster than a frustrating experience in attempting to apply a newly learned principle.

Organization

While not as organized as direct instruction, semi-direct instruction must still be a fairly well-organized type of presentation if it is to succeed. The instructor maintains control of the flow of the instruction by the questions asked, as in a case study, or by the procedural outline provided, as in demonstration/performance.

The primary organizational vehicle for semi-direct instruction will be the instructional objective. For example, the purpose of a case study session may be to be able to evaluate the use of various computerized data bases for different purposes. All activities during the instruction then point to that end. The organization of the instruction focuses on that objective, and the students need to be aware of what that objective is from the very beginning, so they can tie all the class activities to it.

In a demonstration/performance session, the organization is provided by the model of the procedure given during the demonstration. Steps need to be clearly delineated and highlighted so that the organization of the procedure is clear and the students can follow it easily.

In these types of semi-direct instruction and all other variations of it, a good organizational method is the provision of periodic summaries during the instruction. They will help to highlight important points which have been made and sometimes obscured by the way this type of instruction proceeds. Summaries also tie concepts together so that the lesson's organizational structure becomes clearer. Therefore, the instructor should make an attempt to insert periodic summaries when using semi-direct instruction.

Active Responding
This principle of learning is a basic component of semi-direct instruction, and therefore, the instructor need not worry too much about producing opportunities for active responding. The main concern will be with guiding those responses to maximize the learning and providing all the students with opportunities to respond. In the use of a case study, the guidance comes from the type and sequence of questions the instructor asks. For demonstration/performance, the guidance comes from the model initially presented and the instructions given during the performance phase. With each method, the instructor needs to have carefully dissected the responses the students will need to make to get the

most out of the experience and then set the stage, either through questions or through procedural outlines, to be sure that the students cover each of the critical steps in the process and recognize them for what they are.

Feedback

Because there is ample opportunity for active responding in semi-direct instruction and because the instructor maintains a fair degree of structure in the situation, there is also ample opportunity for feedback to occur. In case study instruction, the feedback comes from the instructor in the way he or she responds to students' answers to questions. In demonstration/performance, the instructor is less likely to be able to watch over each student's shoulder to provide feedback. Therefore, the instructor must rely on the consequences of the environment ("Did the machine work or not?"), well-defined tasks with preset answers ("If you did this right, you should have gotten the following answer"), or other students ("Did your partner follow all the steps? Did the answer make sense to you?"). However, the instructor should be available during the performance phase and should circulate to provide whatever feedback is possible.

As we discussed earlier, summaries provide a good source of feedback for this type of instruction, too. When the case has been dissected or the performance completed, the instructor should provide a debriefing which includes a discussion of the common problems and successes the students had in dealing with the material and ties all the instruction up into a neat package. This debriefing will bring the instruction to a satisfactory close and suggest how the students can extrapolate what they have learned to the real world.

Indirect Instruction

Motivation

For indirect instruction, the source of motivation comes from the fact that the students are actively involved in the learning. The activities in which they are engaged are usually very relevant and practical. There is usually very little need for the instructor to do anything additional to motivate the learners other than to be certain that the activities are relevant and that there is ample opportunity for the students to see they are successful in the assigned task. For example, in the case of a discussion class, most students like to hear themselves talk, to share their experiences, and to find that others have similar experiences. In addition, the instructor leading the discussion will be listening attentively and responding supportively to their comments, which is another source of motivation.

Organization

Although indirect instruction is strong in motivation, it is definitely weak in organization. It is here that the instructor must put forth the greatest effort to see to it that this principle is followed. Indirect instruction is unorganized only in that it is impossible to predict with one hundred percent accuracy the direction the students will take during the course of their learning. The instructor must be able to adapt to whatever direction they lead and still be able to tie things together with the main point of the instruction.

The primary vehicle for the provision of organization in indirect instruction is the debriefing. During the debriefing, which occurs at the end of the simulation or discussion, the instructor summarizes what has occurred, highlighting main ideas and explaining the processes which brought the students to the final point. This requires that the instructor has paid close attention to what went on during the discussion, simulation, etc., and can pull it all together into a coherent package. Failure to do this will leave the students with little of which they can be certain as a result of the session.

Active Responding

Even more than semi-direct instruction, indirect methods are based on active responding on the part of the learner. Therefore, there is little the instructor need do to enhance this learning principle. The only caution here is to provide all the students with an opportunity to actively respond and not allow some students to dominate the group.

There are many ways of increasing the participation of students. For example, group size makes a big difference. If the instructor decides to break the large group down into smaller groups to encourage participation by everyone, it is wise not to have groups larger than five. Some students are able to hide in groups larger than that size, but it is hard to hide in a group of five or fewer.

Earlier we discussed incorporating sufficient thinking time into a class to allow students to respond to or ask questions. This is particularly important for the more reticent students. Many of those students fail to respond because they have a tendency to think an answer out carefully before volunteering, while other students jump right in and volunteer without thinking. By the time the more reticent students get ready to respond, the others have already answered. Therefore, enforced thinking will help those students become more involved.

Finally, clear definitions of what the students are supposed to be doing are important in indirect instruction because the instructor will not be there to guide their activity. The activity must be able to stand on its own with little or no instructor assistance.

Feedback

Oddly enough, even though there is ample opportunity for active responding in indirect instruction, there is a problem with giving adequate feedback. Since one of the assumptions underlying indirect instruction is that the students are teaching themselves and learning from one another rather than from the instructor, too frequent instructor intervention will defeat the purpose of this type of instruction. The instructor is there to function as a resource person and process observer rather than as a director of behavior. Therefore, all feedback must be delayed until the debriefing if the students are to be allowed to teach themselves.

This delay is one of the distinct disadvantages of indirect instruction. It must stand on its own with very little outside feedback until the end, and then it is often difficult for the students to remember all that went on and how certain comments made during the debriefing relate to what occurred during the learning. In discussion classes, feedback from the instructor is directed most at encouraging students to say something rather than trying to give extensive feedback on the accuracy of what they say. Therefore, while it is more immediate than feedback in other indirect instructional settings, it is often as vague or unconnected to the learning.

In situations like these, the instructor should rely on the debriefing for most content-related feedback. The instructor will need to pay close attention to what occurs during the discussion or simulation or other learning so that specific comments can be made to highlight appropriate and inappropriate responses when the debriefing occurs. If, on the other hand, time is a factor and you don't mind violating the principle of non-interference, especially during a discussion, careful feedback can be given during the learning, mostly in the form of probing questions to help the students identify their own errors.

IN SUMMARY

From the above discussion, you can see that there are four very simple principles of learning to keep in mind when designing and carrying out instruction. They are motivation, organization, active responding, and feedback. Each instructional setting needs to incorporate some aspect of each of them in order to maximize learning. We have also seen that the three different types of instruction we are examining incorporate more or less of each of these principles into their structures. The effective instructor then makes an effort to enhance any of the four principles not inherent in the instruction to the end that all four receive some attention.

At this point, however, much of what we have discussed remains fairly theoretical. Now we need to see how these principles combine to aid in the design of real instruction.

6
Applying the Design Process

Up to this point, we have been discussing the design process on a fairly theoretical level, using examples to illustrate independent components of the process. In this chapter, we will describe eight cases that use the design process to create possibilities for instruction. As in real situations, they are complex, and it is likely that sometimes the logic will seem a bit convoluted; nevertheless, the cases should make interesting reading and show how a little creative thought can make instruction more varied than you might have considered before.

CASE ONE

In a junior-level course in urban planning, the instructor is going to give an assignment in which the students are to "research some aspect of policy in which they are interested and write a ten-page paper which makes recommendations." This assignment is similar to the one he has given for the last two years, and the librarians were very familiar with the panicked looks on the faces of the students in past semesters as they tried to cope with this very nebulous assignment. This year the instructor has decided that the poor quality of papers he's been getting was a result of students' ignorance of library resources, and therefore, he has asked one of the librarians to "give a class presentation on what's available on city planning in the library." There are twenty-five students in the class. It meets three times a week for fifty minutes per session. The instructor is willing to give one class period over to the librarian.

The librarian cleverly recognizes the futility of trying to provide the students with all that information without giving them some ways of sorting through it all. She also realizes that, based on past experience, one of their initial problems was the open-ended nature of the assignment; either the instructor needs to focus it more or the students need to learn something about topic narrowing so that they are able to select resources efficiently.

An initial suggestion might be to get the instructor to spend some time helping the students cope with the expansive nature of the assignment. For example, the librarian might discuss with the instructor how often students have difficulty with this broad an assignment and the increased efficiency of students' library work once they have settled on a narrowed topic. The instructor might at that point choose to restrict the assignment to certain types of problems or provide some topics from which students would be free to choose. However, there are many instructors who resist placing restrictions on students' choices, believing that students are more likely to do better work on topics that interest them. This point is, of course, very valid, but students often flounder when faced with the task of choosing and narrowing a topic in a field in which they have little or no background.

The librarian might suggest that the instructor spend some class time helping the students learn to narrow their topics, possibly by using the topic-narrowing procedure described in Chapter 3. Or if the instructor resists giving over class time to this process, the librarian might prepare a handout on topic narrowing which the instructor could distribute along with the assignment or in the period before the librarian is to conduct class. Any of these techniques could alleviate part of the students' problems by giving them a clearer focus for their research activities. The narrowed topics could then be used while the librarian is in the class to crystallize what is being discussed.

In order to decide what activities should be included in the librarian's class session, we should go back through our design procedure to determine what might be acceptable. Once all restrictions have been considered, we should have some ideas about what to do in class.

Step One: The Objectives

The first step in planning this instruction is to decide what the appropriate objective or objectives for the session are. We begin with a need to interpret the instructor's request for "what's available on city planning in the library." What would such a statement mean in terms of student achievement?

One possibility is the following: "what's available" equals "students will be able to list potential resources on city planning." But, of course, the librarian knows that the instructor means to imply more than this statement and that there is more to the students' deficits in research than simply a lack of knowledge of what sources are available.

In reality, the instructor probably intends the following:

MAIN OBJECTIVE: Students will synthesize information drawn from a variety of urban planning sources representing the breadth and depth of sources available.

After all, it was his dissatisfaction with students' research, as evidenced in their papers, which caused the instructor to seek the librarian's input.

It might be useful for the librarian to discuss with the instructor what he considers to be the students' greatest weaknesses. Such a discussion could have several benefits. First, what the instructor is being critical of might differ from the librarian's interpretation of "poor use of resources." He may mean that insufficient sources are cited or that sources are used to support inaccurate conclusions. The librarian can usually help with the former, but only the instructor can deal with the latter. If there is a difference of interpretation, the librarian could be saved a great deal of time and anguish by finding it out beforehand. In addition, the instructor may be able to identify particular types of errors to which students are likely to fall prey. The librarian, being aware of these errors, can take steps to correct them more efficiently by highlighting potential trouble spots early. A side benefit of this discussion could be an increase in the instructor's awareness of the role played by library research in the quality of papers. This might encourage him to pay closer attention to that aspect of the assign-

ment. The librarian may be able to contribute some valuable in-
sights into what the students should be able to accomplish.

The librarian also knows that the main objective entails more
than library skills, and her task is to derive from it relevant objectives that will focus her instruction. The main objective implies
that the students must be made aware, if they are not already, of
the differences in quality among different types of sources, how
different sources are appropriate for different audiences, and how
to distinguish among them. Therefore, some library skills objectives that should be included with the main objective are the following:

1) Students will be able to list the variety of sources available
on urban planning.
2) Students will be able to describe the type of information
available from each source, in terms of complexity, sophistication, and purpose.
3) Students will be able to match support materials with their
topic and their level of sophistication.

The first two in this group are basic information-type objectives. The first objective asks only that students be able to list
what is available; the second asks for a description of the information available in each source. Either of these two could be
achieved through simple memorization. The third objective is an
intermediate application of skills. It requires that the students be
able to manipulate the information about sources. That manipu-
lation is in the form of being able to tell the difference between
two different sources in terms of their use.

In thinking about objectives one and two, we can see that
there is no reason for the students to memorize the information
at this time as long as they know that it exists, that different
sources contain different information, and that more details about

the sources are available if needed. Eventually, as students do more and more work in the field, certain sources will become very familiar; for now, however, all they really need is a convenient place to find a list of sources that is organized in a way which facilitates their use. These objectives are basic cognitive objectives, and if we look at Figure 4.1 again, we see that we can select a direct format which will provide that content. Referring back to our continuum (Figure 2.1), we find the options for direct instruction: We can provide information and the organizational structure in a mini-lecture and the detailed information about each source in printed material which the students will be able to use later. Our purpose here is only to get across the idea that there are many sources and where to find them.

Objective three is an application of these ideas to the selection of sources for a given use. Because it is an intermediate application of skills, this objective requires a more participative format. Referring back to our continuum, we find that we could choose either demonstration/performance, case study, or even some of the small-group synergogic designs for this application because they are all semi-direct methods of instruction. The key is employing some method which will give the students an opportunity to apply the concepts of source differences and selection. This will provide both a better learning situation and a more enjoyable session for the group.

Step Two: The Students

Now let's consider the students. Is there anything about them that would influence our selection of teaching methods? Because this is a junior-level class, we can assume some exposure to a variety of reading materials, though not necessarily in this discipline; their exposure is more likely going to be in general resources more readily accessible to the public such as magazines, newspapers, and

Readers' Guide, rather than in scholarly material such as journals or specialized indexes in this field. Therefore, the students could be considered to have "some" background in the content. However, they are more sophisticated than beginning students in terms of the type of material they are accustomed to learning and probably in their general thinking and study skills. Their abilities would probably put the class in the "some" to "a lot" range of learning skills. Therefore, we can be comfortable in restricting any direct presentation of content to overviews and providing detailed information in printed format, allowing them to learn more on their own. This approach frees time for participation and allows them to contribute to the class, something more mature students appreciate.

The motivation level of the students will be moderate because they have an assignment to complete in the near future. The timing allows the librarian to focus the instruction on meeting their needs more closely. The more closely the connection is made, the more motivated they will be to listen and learn. However, being upper-division students may make them feel that they know more than they do, so the instruction will need to be interesting and challenging as well as give them adequate opportunity to see how it applies to their own work.

Given these student characteristics, we can safely use some of the more student-controlled methods without too much concern because our students would seem to be sophisticated enough and motivated enough to handle some semi-direct or indirect instruction. If we refer back to our chart on the relationship of student characteristics and teaching methods (Figure 4.1), we see that for more sophisticated students, semi-direct and indirect methods are preferred. Any direct instruction should be kept to a minimum or made into something the learner can use individually.

Step Three: The Situation

From the standpoint of situational constraints, the number of students (twenty-five) is not excessive, so from Figure 4.1 we can see that just about any method is appropriate. Time restrictions (fifty minutes) will be a problem: The fifty-minute limit would lead us toward direct instruction and away from indirect. However, semi-direct, which requires a little more time than direct but less than indirect, might be a possibility. If we remind ourselves that with learners at this level, there is no need to cover *all* the content during the class, we could get around the time constraints. We should concentrate on helping the students learn the skills that will enable them to exploit the resources available for self-help later. These few skills—such as how to select a likely source for information—would be better taught through semi-direct methods. While semi-direct methods are initially more time-consuming, focusing on the skills now would save time in the long run, when the students actually begin trying to use the literature.

Because the session will be conducted in the classroom, it would be cumbersome to use the real reference materials, so we may have to find acceptable substitutes with which students can work. These might be mock copies of the specialized reference materials designed to contain all the relevant parts for understanding how the real volume is arranged. Or the actual sources may have little or no meaning to the students at this point, and the librarian can leave out that part of the presentation. We'll probably need a chalkboard and an overhead projector, both of which are likely to be available, though the librarian may wish to check with the instructor on the latter.

One obstacle that often faces instructors is the seating arrangement in a room. Most classrooms are arranged for the benefit of the cleaning staff: all chairs and desks in a row, facing front where there is a podium or desk which may impede access to the chalkboard. This particular room arrangement creates many problems for instructors. In the first place, it makes group work more difficult because students can't easily turn and work together. The best way to overcome this obstacle is to rearrange the room if you can, or if the chairs are bolted to the floor, keep group work small or short. Small groups (two or three) are not too difficult to organize even in a very restrictive classroom setting; larger groups (five and over) require students to get up and move around in order to hear and be heard. The latter arrangement can work if the students don't have to be up and around very long, although the movement is very time-consuming. The small group size is usually adequate for most tasks which a librarian would be doing during a class period.

In addition to being inconvenient for group activity, the standard classroom setting works psychologically against active learning and student independence. In a standard classroom, there is one focal point for attention: the front of the room where the instructor stands. This sets the information emanating from that point apart for special consideration. To some, it implies that there is one correct answer and the instructor has it. Therefore, injecting variety into the classroom setting might serve to encourage the students to stop thinking of the instructor as the fountain of all knowledge and begin to accept their own place in the scheme of learning.

This digression into classroom dynamics was made only to suggest that even though this classroom may be in a standard set-up, it could be worthwhile to violate the expectations created by the room arrangement in order to achieve some valid instructional purpose. Fortunately, with this class, the small number of students makes many things possible.

Step Four: The Instructor

At this point in the design process, the librarian would normally consider how her skills might affect the choice of instructional method. Since we don't actually have a real person to analyze in this book, let us consider what skills would be necessary to deal with the potential methods we are considering.

Since it is likely that there will be at least some direct instruction during the period, the librarian will need some presentation skills, particularly those having to do with organizing information to give the overall picture. These skills will play a role in preparing the handouts on available resources and in presenting the brief lecture explaining how resources are organized. Perhaps one of the most critical yet subtle skills during this presentation will be resisting the temptation to tell the students everything, practically repeating the handouts and thus defeating the organizational function of the presentation.

Another important set of skills the librarian will need will be facilitating and orchestrating during any periods in which the students are attempting to work in small groups. These skills involve being able to give clear directions on what to look for without telling the students what to find. They also require that the librarian be able to ask students to contribute their ideas and to provide encouraging feedback when appropriate responses are offered and correcting feedback when the ideas offered are not appropriate. Semi-direct and indirect methods also require that the librarian be able to listen closely to the students' ideas and pull them together into a coherent whole periodically throughout the session. The ability to summarize and point the way for further work is critical to the smooth functioning of student group work. The ability to respond genuinely to students' contributions is another skill important to semi-direct and indirect methods. Since so much of the learning requires students to carry out the assigned task, the instructor's role is greatly changed from information dispenser to encourager and sounding board. Sometimes this is a difficult role change for instructors to accept.

If our hypothetical librarian is lacking any of these characteristics, she may need to choose an alternative method or think of some way of providing the benefits of a particular method without actually doing that component herself. For example, if the librarian is not a good presenter, the printed materials may need to be all that much better to compensate. Or if the librarian has difficulty summarizing, she may prepare a tentative list of major points which hopefully will be raised during discussion and then check them off as they come up. Then when it's time for a summary, she can consult this list, noting aloud the points that were made and adding those that were left out. Alternatively, one of the students might be appointed to carry out this function prior to the open discussion. The librarian would then simply confirm the accuracy of that summary and add to it.

Intermission: Taking Stock of Teaching Options

At this point, we have several possibilities, as we see in Figure 6.1. Based on our objectives, we have need for some direct instruction to provide the details of what resources are available, and we have some semi-direct instruction which would give the students practice in matching source materials to possible topics and their own needs. The learners don't place any serious restrictions on what we can choose, other than to encourage us to restrict direct instruction and allow more participation.

Situational constraints are something to consider, primarily because of time restrictions. In this case, there is not much time available, which would push us toward direct instruction, but for-

Constraint		Teaching Options
Objectives	List sources - Basic Describe sources - Basic Match sources - Intermediate	Direct Direct Semi-direct
Students	Juniors Somewhat sophisticated learners Some exposure to materials Motivation moderate	Can handle semi-direct or indirect
Situation	Small class Time limited No access to resources Class arrangement a problem	Direct or semi-direct

Figure 6.1 Constraint analysis for Case One.

tunately the sophistication of our learners gives us an out. They have the capability of using material on their own, and there is no real pressing need to get all the detailed information across during this particular class period.

As noted earlier, the room situation might also pose a challenge. If the arrangement is standard, which is likely, we'll want to be careful to keep any group exercises small or short.

Class size is no problem, but resources might be tricky. Since the instruction will take place in the classroom rather than in the library, ready access to the actual resource materials may not be possible, so the need for them may have to be restricted or clever substitutes will need to be made.

Step Five: Sequencing Instruction

Now that we've looked at the restrictions we need to consider, we would envision a Kolb cycle to see how we can sequence the in-

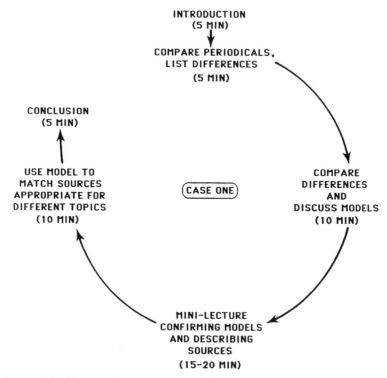

Figure 6.2   Instructional sequence for Case One.

struction. Follow along with Figure 6.2 as we structure the class period around Kolb's cycle. Should it begin with "experience" or "explanation"?

We don't have the time or facilities to actually give the learners a concrete experience, but we are fortunate enough to have somewhat sophisticated learners who may already have enough experience that we can draw on quickly to allow us to start at the experience phase. To communicate the idea that there are different levels of sources appropriate for various uses (a component of objective three), we could begin with an exercise that asks pairs of students to compare a scholarly article published in an urban-planning journal with an article on the same topic published in a popular magazine and list the differences. This type of activity is similar to the semi-direct method of performance-judging and is aimed at making the students aware of criteria that can be used to choose among sources, a skill they will be applying later when looking at resources for their papers.

Once the pairs have completed their lists (experience phase of the cycle), the class as a whole compares the lists of various groups and attempts to synthesize their conclusions into a model for judging materials. The librarian prompts them with questions such as "Which article has a bibliography at the end?" or "What does each publication tell you about the author's credentials?" as needed. Synthesizing the lists of the smaller groups causes the students to reflect on the statements they've made about their own experiences with these sources, which is "examination," the second phase of the cycle.

At this point, the librarian confirms the group's findings in a mini-lecture and generalizes the concept (popular vs. scholarly) to the sources students might use for their papers. The content of this lecture would reiterate the idea that materials vary in their quality, as the students have just confirmed by their own experience. The librarian ties that idea to the concept of general and specialized periodical indexes. She then lists on the board titles of several indexes and some of the periodicals covered by each. The librarian's comments draw students' attention to a handout which lists the indexes available to them in terms of whatever criteria are appropriate for their purposes. For example, the breakdown might be according to level of sophistication of sources covered by an index or according to discipline. Whatever the divisions of the printed material, the purpose of the lecture would be to highlight the structure of the division and emphasize that the printed material can be used later when deciding what resources to consult.

Because these students have some but not a lot of background using these specific sources, it is necessary to use direct instruction to accomplish this basic objective of information transfer on the variety of resources available (objective one). As noted earlier, it would be best to provide detailed information appropriate to objective two in printed format to save time, to respect the sophistication level of the learners, and to keep the in-class time focused on process and application rather than information transfer. During the mini-lecture, therefore, the librarian's goal would be to generalize from the familiar materials the students have just considered to the unfamiliar materials with which they will be working and then to describe how the students can use the printed handouts to make the same kind of discriminations among the more specialized sources. This lecture constitutes the explanation phase of the cycle, in which the students come to understand the underlying model for evaluating information sources.

To give the learners practice in making these discriminations, the librarian could then move on to the application phase in the sequence and have the learners practice selecting from their list of sources those that would be appropriate for different topics. For example, the librarian might propose a hypothetical case in which a student is writing a report for a citizen's advisory group, urging them to adopt a wastewater treatment plan involving hyacinths. The students would be asked to identify from their lists which sources would be useful in various sections of the paper. After two or three examples, the librarian could have students identify the type of materials that would be good resources for their own topics.

Step Six: Checking for Continuity with Learning Principles

Now we return to our set of objectives. Have we included them all? The third objective is "the students will be able to match sup-

port materials with their topic and their level of sophistication."
The last exercise described above was designed to give practice in
that. Our other objectives were that the student would be able to
list sources and describe the information available in them; these
objectives were achieved with a combination of printed material
and a mini-lecture on how to use it.

How would these activities be timed in class? Figure 6.2
shows how the cycle might be completed in a fifty- to sixty-
minute period. Note that much less time than usual is spent in direct instruction; about half the session is spent in active student
learning. Laid out in this fashion, the segments seem short, but the
amount of activity and variety of activities should keep the class's
attention and keep the students working. Compare this scenario
in your mind with a fifty-minute lecture on alternative sources of
information, which would probably seem to drag, both to the
audience and to the presenter. In which scenario would more
learning occur?

If we ask this question from the standpoint of the learning
principles discussed in Chapter 5, there is not much doubt that
our proposed methods would result in more learning in the long
run. The procedures we have included focus students' attention directly on the materials they are going to use in situations that are
identical to those in which they will soon find themselves. The
class session even ends with students working on their own paper
topics. This should enhance the motivation value of the presentation. In addition, since so much of the time is spent in active use
of the concepts being learned, the students should benefit from
that principle of learning as well. Of course, inherent in that active
learning is the opportunity for feedback.

The one area where the librarian will have to be especially
conscious of emphasis is that of organization. Here we are refer-

ring to the organization of the material to be learned. The bulk of this organization comes in the mini-lecture component and from the layout of the printed materials. The librarian will need to take care to tie what the students do in the active participation periods of the class to the organizational structure illustrated in the lecture and printed material.

Thus we have taken the case as originally outlined and come up with one potential hour session to help students understand the use of the wide range of resources potentially available to them. We began by first analyzing the constraints placed on the teaching by the objectives, the students, the situation, and the instructor. Then we considered how some of our potential methods might fit into a learning cycle. Finally we checked the plan for adherence to learning principles and found a fairly satisfactory match. Let us emphasize, however, that this is only one of several possible instructional sequences which might have resulted from our deliberations. Shifts in any of these variables could significantly alter what could be done in class.

Let's consider the process again with a different situation.

CASE TWO

Unlike our previous case in which an instructor approached the librarian for assistance with a particular assignment, in this case the librarian is faced with a need for instruction that the library staff has created. They have just installed an on-line catalog system which library users can now employ to do most of the things they previously did with the card catalog. The staff must now provide training for anyone who wishes to use the system. The question is, what is the best method for providing this training?

Step One: The Objectives

Once again, we begin by assessing the objective of the instruction. Stated in simple terms, the overall objective would be the following:

> The user will be able to use the on-line catalog to complete any function that was possible with the card catalog.

The key word is "use," which implies application, an intermediate-level objective. Going back to our earlier discussions, we find that whenever the instruction involves learning a skill, the preferred methods are semi-direct. Therefore, in this case, we would choose among demonstration/performance, case study, computer-assisted instruction, and so on.

An important point to note is that it is not the purpose of this training to teach the use of the card catalog; we will be assuming a familiarity with those skills. For the user requiring training in the use of the card catalog, some other unit of instruction would be appropriate. Our only objective is to teach the use of the on-line catalog, to transfer what the learner already knows about finding a book or books over to the new system. Therefore, there is no need to consider other methods; we need only choose from among semi-direct methods.

Step Two: The Students

This case presents an interesting twist with regard to the students for whom this instruction is intended. They are essentially faceless and hard to characterize because they are anyone who would use the card catalog and who is not "technophobic" and, therefore, reluctant to try the computer as a substitute for the old system. If, however, we would be dealing with technophobic individuals who no longer had the option of using the card catalog, we would have quite a different task, since that would add an affective component to our instruction. We would not only have to teach them to use the on-line catalog, but also overcome their reluctance to do so. For now, however, we will assume they still have a choice, and our only task is to provide instruction for those who are already interested in using the on-line catalog.

About all we can say for certain about these potential learners is that they have a background in using the card catalog. We are not sure how sophisticated that background might be, but it would probably be safe to assume some minimal set of skills and knowledge about how the catalog is used and organized, perhaps only to the extent of knowing that each book can be found by looking up its title or author and that part of the catalog lists books by subject. Additionally, the users would know at a basic level the significance of the call number associated with each entry.

As far as familiarity with computers is concerned, it would be best not to assume anything. It is not the purpose of this instruction to teach the user anything about the computer itself, just as it would not be our purpose to teach the user of a card catalog how to open the drawers that hold the cards. The drawer or the terminal should be arranged in such a way that its use is self-explanatory. It would be up to the programmer and the terminal designer to make any technical understanding of the computer itself unnecessary.

What else can we deduce about our faceless learner? The librarian would need to be familiar with the library's probable clientele. Users of the card catalog would be likely to have some educational background, but to assume extensive learning skills would be risky. It would be just as foolish to assume none, so we are safe in expecting our learners to have some learning skills, at least to the point of following simple directions. Otherwise they would be unlikely to be consulting the card catalog in the first place.

One thing we know for sure about our learners is that they are motivated to learn to use this new procedure because the training is for "anyone who wishes it." That is not to say we needn't concern ourselves with motivation. However, our concern will be more for helping learners see progress rapidly enough to satisfy their immediate desire to learn than for trying to convince them to learn in the first place.

Step Three: The Situation

The decision variables in this case revolve much more around the situational constraints, specifically the number of learners and the timing of instruction. It would not be feasible or desirable to do this type of training in group settings, except perhaps for the library staff. Attempts to provide group training and still meet the criterion of having training available when the user wants it would mean having regularly scheduled training sessions available all the time. The logistics of such sessions are hopelessly complex; they would mean making library staff available without any guarantee that users would find scheduled times convenient. Both users and staff find such arrangements inconvenient, particularly if the training were to extend over long periods of time. With library staff, of course, the training could be concentrated into a few periods and schedules adjusted on a one-time basis to accommodate the training. But even with the library staff, the probable number of terminals available at a single time would severely limit group size.

The consideration of actual time required by the instruction itself is something the librarian needs to be sensitive to. Learners who want to use the on-line catalog probably assume it will save them time and effort. Therefore, the time involved in learning to use it should not exceed what they would have spent at the card catalog. To allow for differences in temperament and patience of the learners, the librarian should let the learner have control over how much time he or she spends trying to master the system. This will permit very compulsive or insecure learners to spend lots of time on it, while less patient learners can satisfy their immediate needs and learn more later.

Other situational constraints would be the equivalent of classroom setup and resources. If the training is to be at the convenience of the user, then the training setting must be available and accessible whenever the library is open. Since the instruction will probably not be done in a group, there are actually few constraints here other than making it obvious where training can be obtained and possibly stationing the terminals near a regularly-staffed work area to provide backup, should questions arise.

In cases like this, the most logical alternative would be individual, semi-direct instruction and, for obvious reasons, computer-assisted instruction would be the best choice. Not only does it fit the needs of the objective and situational constraints, but it is additional practice with the very technology we are trying to teach. However, this method does require sufficient equipment to accommodate training needs without interfering with actual catalog use.

Step Four: The Instructor
Since the instruction is to be done on a self-study basis, interaction and presentation skills are not instructor skills needed in this case. Here the instructor is primarily an organizer and designer of instruction rather than a deliverer of the instruction. Therefore, the most desirable skills here are those of being able to put oneself in the shoes of the learners to anticipate what questions and problems they will have, to sift out key concepts and sequence them in a way which will make sense, and to provide examples and activities which will help the learners progress smoothly. While

these qualities are desirable in any teaching situation, they are particularly important in individual instruction designed to function autonomously. In all other cases, the instructor is present to make on-the-spot adjustments as problems arise. Designers of individual learning systems do not have that luxury, but must anticipate and plan around problems so they never arise in the first place. That is why most instruction intended for individual use is reviewed by several individuals and field-tested before being used. The multiple perspectives of the design team preclude many of the problems which might surface if only one person was involved in the design.

It should also be noted that it is not necessary to have computer-programming skills in order to use computer-assisted instruction. Most CAI programs are joint projects between the instructional designer, a content specialist, and the programmer. There are very few instructors who would have the programming facility to write something of the complexity implied by a good instructional program. Therefore, most people hire someone else to do the actual coding and they take responsibility for the outline and content of the program.

Intermission: Taking Stock of Teaching Options

At this point, given the variables summarized in Figure 6.3, we have essentially settled on the instructional method: computer-assisted instruction in the form of demonstration/performance. The task now is to design the modular sequence itself so that it takes advantage of what we have discussed about learning and sequencing instruction. The choice of demonstration/performance satisfies the objectives of our situation, while the choice of individual rather than group instruction satisfies some of the situational needs we are confronted with in terms of timing and distribution of audience. The learner constraints do not hinder the

Constraint		Teaching Options
Objectives	Use catalog - Intermediate	Semi-direct
Students	Some background in card catalog Some learning skills Good motivation	Semi-direct
Situation	Large number of potential learners On-demand instruction Limited number of terminals available Time for learning under control of learners	Individual

Figure 6.3   Constraint analysis for Case Two.

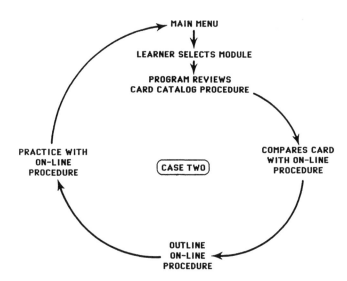

Figure 6.4   Instructional sequence for Case Two.

use of either of these choices, but we must be careful about the structure of the program itself, which we will discuss in the next section. Once again, the instructor constraints we must take into account would probably best be dealt with by using a design team.

Step Five: Sequencing Instruction

To design a computer program which will teach someone to use a skill they already have in a new setting, we intend to follow the model of a demonstration/performance presentation. That would involve briefly illustrating a particular aspect of the skill followed by active practice of that skill by the learner. Figure 6.4 shows how each of the modules might be constructed to follow the Kolb cycle.

```
 _____
|                                                            |
|                                                            |
|                                                            |
|      Which of the following card catalog uses would you    |
|                  like to have illustrated?                 |
|                    (Type letter of choice.)                |
|                                                            |
|        A.  Find an item when I have the author's name.     |
|                                                            |
|        B.  Find an item when I have the title.             |
|                                                            |
|        C.  Find all the items on a given topic.            |
|                                                            |
|        D.  Go directly to use the on-line catalog.         |
|                                                            |
|        E.  Stop the program.                               |
|                                                            |
|                  PRESS RETURN TO CONTINUE                   |
|                                                            |
|_____|
```

Figure 6.5   Screen for main menu.

```
┌─────────────────────────────────────────────────────────┐
│                                                           │
│     TO SEARCH FOR AN ITEM FOR WHICH YOU KNOW              │
│                                                           │
│                   THE TITLE                               │
│     Recall that when you know the title of the item you want │
│                    to find, you:                          │
│              1. consult the author/title catalog          │
│                                                           │
│                        and                                │
│                                                           │
│              2. look alphabetically for the first word    │
│                 of the title, excluding articles ("a," "an," │
│                 and "the").                               │
│     To find the book  The Great Gatsby,  you would look   │
│              1. in the author/title catalog               │
│                                                           │
│              2. under "Great"                             │
│                                                           │
│                PRESS RETURN TO CONTINUE                   │
│                   TYPE "QUIT" TO RETURN TO MENU           │
└─────────────────────────────────────────────────────────┘
```

Figure 6.6   Screen for experiencing phase.

For purposes of illustration, we have created part of a CAI program that could be used in this case. The first screen briefly explains that the purpose of the program is to help users transfer their skills with the card catalog to this new on-line catalog. Then the program displays a list of options (called the main menu) from which the user can choose. As you can see in Figure 6.5, these options are phrased in terms of skills used in dealing with the card catalog, which allows the users to tap into their existing understanding of how to find what they're looking for. If the user chooses one of the first three options, the program begins the actual instruction part of the process. At this point, the user is asked to recall his or her experiences with the card catalog, Figure 6.6, which is the experience phase of the Kolb cycle. Then, in the examination phase, the program asks the user to compare these

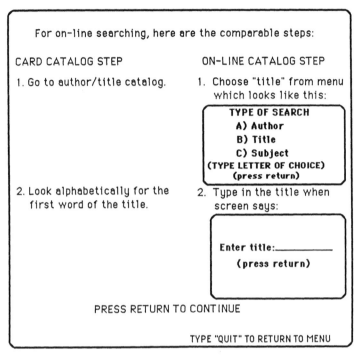

Figure 6.7   Screen for examining phase.

familiar steps with the comparable procedures for the on-line
catalog. Figure 6.7 illustrates the screen that outlines the steps
for each system. Next the program "explains" the steps for using
the on-line catalog and asks the user to verify his or her understanding by responding (Figure 6.8). These responses comprise the
application phase. If the user responds incorrectly, the program
corrects the user and repeats the previous screen. If the user responds correctly, the program moves on to the next step (Figure
6.9).

At this point, the program responds according to the appropriateness of the user's response. If the response is correct, the
user is allowed to try a few more applications with a variety of

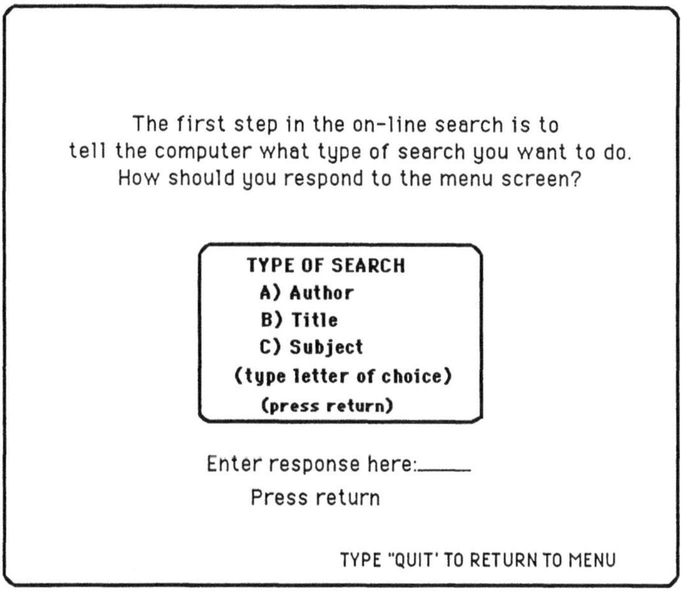

```
        The first step in the on-line search is to
    tell the computer what type of search you want to do.
        How should you respond to the menu screen?


                    TYPE OF SEARCH
                    A) Author
                    B) Title
                    C) Subject
                    (type letter of choice)
                    (press return)

                Enter response here:_____
                Press return

                            TYPE "QUIT' TO RETURN TO MENU
```

Figure 6.8 First screen for explaining and applying phase.

other titles which might be confusing, such as journals. At the bottom of each screen are the instructions for stopping the tutorial and returning to the main menu. From the main menu, the user could try another skill or go to an actual search with the real data base.

The other two types of searches (author and subject) would be structured in the same format in terms of responses a user must make. If the information provided by the screen which displays the data about a particular entry is significantly different from what the users would expect in the card catalog, one might also need to include a module on how to read a screen entry. It would be most desirable to make the actual on-line catalog as similar to the card catalog as is feasible, so that there is direct transfer of the ability to read a card in the card catalog to the ability to read an

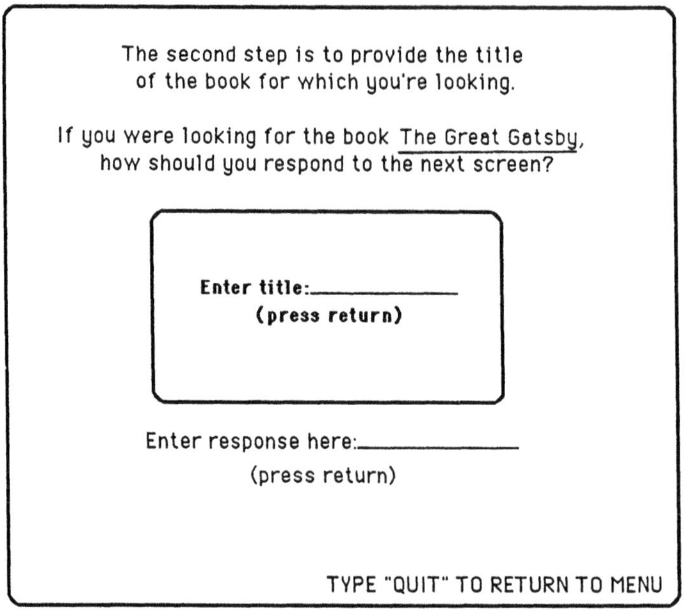

The second step is to provide the title
of the book for which you're looking.

If you were looking for the book The Great Gatsby,
how should you respond to the next screen?

Enter title:_____
(press return)

Enter response here:_____
(press return)

TYPE "QUIT" TO RETURN TO MENU

Figure 6.9   Second screen for explaining and applying phase.

entry on the screen. In addition, the actual on-line catalog should
have instructions on every screen which explain to the user how to
go on to more entries or to return to the main menu. If the on-
line catalog is not set up this way, the instructional program
should review these procedures. The key to designing this type of
user-friendly computer system is to parallel as closely as possible
the way the user would have used the card catalog itself. This will
minimize the amount of actual training necessary.

Step Six: Checking for Continuity with Learning Principles

How does the procedure just outlined use the learning principles
of Chapter 5? If we begin with motivation, there are two places
where it is considered. In the first place, our choice of individual

instruction allows us to take advantage of the motivation inherent in the immediate needs of the users. *They* are the ones who *choose* to engage in the learning at their convenience because the instruction is available when they need it. Second, the program is organized in small, easy-to-master steps, thus ensuring success. This success serves as a motivator for continued learning. At the same time, the opportunity to stop whenever the user chooses is built into the program. This helps to avoid frustration if the user is having problems. It seems that computer-assisted instruction has covered the area of motivation fairly well.

Organization is sometimes a problem in a computer-assisted instructional sequence. The format of this program tries to heighten the user's awareness of the organization inherent in the structure of the on-line catalog and thus avoid that problem. First, the program is broken down into small modules corresponding to the three types of searches possible. This small number of modules is a very logical division of the content and is based on the most common uses of the card catalog; this highlights the organization and, more important, bases it on an organizational structure with which the users are already familiar. As we saw earlier, this approach saves a lot of time in learning. Then, too, within each module the program bases the learning of the new procedures on the user's understanding of the old procedures of the card catalog. This approach also saves time by tapping into previously learned material.

An important contributing factor to the use of organization in the learning of the on-line catalog would be the organization of the catalog itself. As mentioned earlier, it is important in the design of the on-line catalog to make it as similar as possible to the organization of the user's existing system for accessing the information. If, for some technical reason, this is not possible, then the training will have to be expanded to include training in the new organizational system. Such training would be a much more difficult task than the one we have set out here and cannot be treated in this brief case. It is important, therefore, that the librarians responsible for instruction pay close attention to what is going into the structure of an on-line catalog in order to direct its development if they can or to be prepared for the confusion users might experience if the catalog is designed to the specifications of the machine rather than the user.

The requirement for active responding and rapid feedback is inherent in the structure of a computer-assisted program in principle. The user must make some response to advance the program to the next concept. It is important, however, that this active response be something more than simply "electronic page turning." It was necessary to include two page-turning responses in the above program on those screens which were simply providing information. However, it was important to have meaningful responses included at the application phase. Here the user had to make some decision based on the information which had been provided and apply that information to his or her response. This is what is meant by active response. Granted the response is not all that complex, but its simplicity is due primarily to the fact that this particular skill is not all that complex either. In fact, a really well-designed on-line catalog would probably be so self-evident that instruction would be unnecessary. The hardest part would be finding the correct keys on the terminal, and those could be highlighted with a permanent visual display. The responses which were required in figures 6.8 and 6.9, however, asked the user to verify that he or she understood the required response. Then the feedback would be used to correct any misconceptions or to encourage the user in learning.

It is not surprising that computer-assisted instruction is so closely tied to the learning principles discussed in Chapter 5. This method was, after all, initiated after the articulation of those principles and greatly influenced by them in its infancy. That does not mean, however, that all computer-assisted instruction makes maximum use of learning theory. It can fall short, just as other methods do. This particular example, however, strives to keep the four principles in mind and take advantage of them.

CASE THREE

In a small sophomore science honors class, students are getting their first taste of what it means to write a research-based term paper. The instructor is asking the students to select a theorist or theory representative of one of the themes being studied in class and research some aspect of the scientific, social, or political impact of that person or discovery. Wisely, this instructor realizes that most of these students have not been exposed to the complexities of a university-level research library and will need significant guidance throughout the semester to succeed, even though this is an honors class. She has invited the librarian to work with her to structure a sequence of class sessions and activities that will focus on the research process.

The librarian has a wonderful opportunity in this class because the instructor has not only expressed an interest in having the students learn more than superficially about research but also seems to understand the desirability of spacing that instruction out across the semester, thus indicating an appreciation for the real nature of the research process. Also, since the instructor seems receptive, the librarian has the potential for helping her learn how to teach these skills to the students herself, thus multiplying the impact: That instructor could then apply what she learns to many future classes.

The librarian will probably not need to do much negotiating with the instructor. However, it will be important not to get too carried away and try to include too much instruction in this class to the detriment of the real objectives of the course as a whole. Too much ardor can be as off-putting as not enough. So the librarian should let the instructor lead the way and set the boundaries for instruction in research. This does not mean, however, that the librarian should not make suggestions and push for an appropriate amount of instruction; it simply means that the librarian must keep in mind that even though the instructor is interested in having the students develop library skills, she probably does not intend for them to reach the level of sophistication of a librarian or even a graduate student. It will be the librarian's responsibility to suggest an *appropriate* level of skills for *this* group and then let the instructor decide whether more or less is called for. It might be appropriate for the librarian to give some thought to various levels of use which might be desirable in students at various academic levels. To help explain these differences to the instructor, it would be a good idea to have sample reference lists illustrating various sophistication levels of use. The instructor could indicate what would be desirable and thus clarify her own and the librarian's understanding of what level of instruction to shoot for. Once both understand what is desired, the design process can begin.

Step One: The Objectives

The initial step, of course, is deciding on the objective(s) of this instructional sequence. The ultimate objective is the following:

> The students will be able to use an efficient search strategy to locate sources appropriate for their information needs.

This overall objective is primarily an intermediate-level application objective, although the inclusion of "efficient" and "appropriate" could be interpreted to mean that there are evaluation components which are desired as well. Also implicit in this objective is the more basic objective of knowing what the steps in a search strategy are.

Since the intent in an intermediate cognitive objective of learning is to apply a process, then semi-direct instruction of some sort is probably the most appropriate choice for that portion of the objective. It may be necessary to use a direct instruction method to achieve the basic cognitive objective of knowing the steps of a search strategy. Should the instructor actually want to reach the level of efficient searches, this advanced component might involve some semi-direct or indirect methods in order to give the students practice in differentiating among alternative strategies. Here is where the earlier thought given to desired sophistication level comes into play.

It is almost always possible to teach any procedure at several levels of sophistication. At a beginning level, the learner is given a step-by-step procedure with very little opportunity for deviation, sort of like a "triptik" from the American Automobile Association, which charts out the most efficient path with no choice points. At a higher level of sophistication, some alternative paths are laid out for the traveler, depending on what the immediate needs are at the moment. The traveler makes choices but is still following one of the paths already charted. At the most sophisticated level, a preset path is not indicated, but rather the traveler is given the skills to chart his or her own trip, making informed decisions along the way and gathering the information to make those decisions as the need arises.

The same is true for the search process. The steps can be laid out in a fairly straight line. This might not represent the most elegant or efficient strategy, but rather the path least likely to get lost on. Such a process would require no evaluative effort on the part of the student and, therefore, would be application only. Or the search path might be laid out like a decision tree with recommendations made at each decision point. The student would be required to choose at each point, but once the choice is made the next step would be indicated. This process would require some evaluative skill, but not much; the few decisions made would be among equally useful alternatives. The probability of becoming totally lost would be low. At the upper level of sophistication, the learner is given not a path but a set of decision rules which would help him or her make decisions among all the possibilities to try next and what to do when something doesn't work. Here it would be possible to become totally lost, and therefore, a high level of sophistication is required. Depending on which of these levels the instructor wished to reach, the method of instruction would be either semi-direct or indirect. At this level of class, it would probably be unrealistic to aim for the highest level; most likely the first level would be appropriate with this class because the focus of the course is not really on research skills per se.

Because it is likely that the search strategy will be outlined for the students, it would be appropriate to break down the overall objective into smaller objectives representing the steps in the process and design instruction around each. This finer analysis might result in a list of objectives which would look like the following:

1) Students will be able to list the steps in a search strategy.
2) Students will be able to use background information sources to narrow the topic of their research.
3) Students will be able to use the *Library of Congress Subject Headings* and card catalog to locate books.
4) Students will be able to use general and specialized periodical indexes to locate articles on the topic of choice.

Each of these objectives can become the focus of a single instructional episode during the semester. The first is a basic cognitive objective, while the other three are intermediate cognitive objectives involving learning to "use" some reference tool and each requiring some background basic objectives of knowing what the sources contain. These basic objectives could be handled with printed materials, as in a previous case, or through more detailed instruction, as the librarian chooses. Our focus, in this instance, is on how to use the tools to accomplish a particular task rather than on the tools themselves.

Step Two: The Students

The student variables in this situation provide us with a little less flexibility than in our first case. As the instructor has so wisely pointed out, the students are not likely to be very sophisticated either in terms of library background or learning skills—even though they are honors students—mostly because they are so new to this situation. They will require more guidance than the junior-level class described earlier. As sophomores, these students will probably not be accustomed to much independent work, but, being honors students, would work very well with some guidance from the instructor. Therefore, a semi-direct method would be preferred over either direct or indirect.

It should be noted that they will probably be fairly well-motivated to learn this material for two reasons. First, the library instruction is being tied very closely to their class assignment and will help make it much easier. Second, the instructor's enthusiasm for the content should also be evident to the students. Her willingness to participate in the instruction on research skills will lend a great deal of credibility to the content as well.

Step Three: The Situation

Situationally, this class is in very good shape. Time will not be much of a problem at all because the instructor is willing to devote small segments of time across the semester to this instruction. Those small bits can add up to a significant amount of instruction. The problem will be breaking down the overall search process into logical segments that can be incorporated into the class every other week or so.

Class size is also no problem. Because there are only twenty students, almost any instructional method would be possible. And in terms of classrooms, classes this small are usually scheduled in rooms with flexible seating, which also means any method is possible. The small class size also has implications for the availability of resources as well. It becomes much easier to provide materials or to move the students to the materials if the materials can't be moved. So the size of the class means that very few constraints are placed on the choice of instruction by the situation.

Step Four: The Instructor

Since it seems likely that the course instructor will be doing quite a bit of this instruction, the librarian will need to prepare good materials to help her carry out any parts she might be doing alone. The librarian will also need to be willing to work *with* the instructor on a cooperative basis, allowing her to take the lead but providing guidance and expert and moral support. Sometimes this can be difficult if it appears that the instructor is not doing things the way we would. However, it is important that the librarian be able to share ownership of the instruction and allow the course instructor to conduct sessions as she sees fit, provided the basic objectives are the same and the information is correct.

For those sessions the librarian conducts herself, she will need the types of skills discussed earlier in Chapter 4 under semi-direct instruction because we are most likely going to use that type of method here. These skills will include presentation skills for any parts requiring information delivery plus the ability to ask questions and give adequate feedback during any practice. Being able to build on the students' needs and experiences to highlight main ideas will also come in handy.

The librarian may be visiting the class more than once, so she will have an opportunity to build some rapport with the group and with individuals in the group. This will require being able to project enthusiasm and concern for the group's problems. The same will be true for her relationship with the instructor. Therefore, good interpersonal skills will be needed.

Intermission: Taking Stock of Teaching Options

At this point, as Figure 6.10 indicates, we have an overall objective broken down into at least four components, most of which are intermediate-level cognitive objectives. In addition, we have some basic information which must be available to complete the intermediate objectives. We have students with some background and some learning skills, but not extensive exposure to the possibilities of library research. Their level points to semi-direct instruction as well. The situational constraints are not limiting at all, thus allowing for any type of instruction. The primary instructor skills needed to operate in this situation are those needed for semi-direct instruction plus good interpersonal skills and the ability to create good support materials to assist the course instructor.

It seems that most of the factors we must consider that actually point to a particular instructional method favor semi-direct instruction. None of the other constraints would prevent us from using these methods. Therefore, we can choose from group methods such as demonstration/performance, case studies, or some of

Constraint		Teaching Options
Objectives	Overall - Intermediate to advanced	Semi-direct or indirect
	List steps - Basic	Direct
	Narrow topic - Intermediate	Semi-direct
	Use subject headings and card catalog - Intermediate	Semi-direct
	Use indexes - Intermediate	Semi-direct
Students	Sophomore honors Not much background Not used to independent work but good enough to work under direction Good motivation	Semi-direct
Situation	Small class No time problems	Anything

Figure 6.10 Constraint analysis for Case Three.

the synergogic methods for in-class work, or individual methods such as workbooks or computer-assisted instruction for out-of-class work. In addition, it might be necessary to include some direct instruction to provide background information where the students are lacking familiarity with it.

Step Five: Sequencing Instruction

From a sequencing standpoint, we are dealing with learners who don't have much experience from which to draw and a content area which would be difficult and frustrating to attempt with no background. Therefore, this time we would be better off beginning with the explaining step and some direct instruction before sending students off to struggle with an experience. The sequence being studied here would look like Figure 6.11.

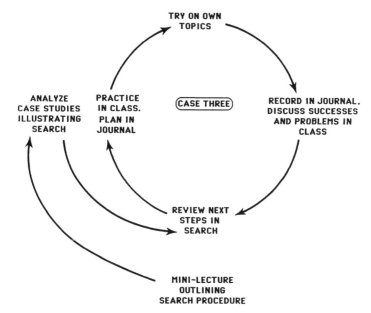

Figure 6.11   Instructional sequence for Case Three.

The initial introduction to the steps of a search strategy could be done by either the course instructor or the librarian, but it would consist of an overview of the process. Then in an application phase, a case study approach could be used to allow the students to try to use the new information in understanding how a search proceeds. The students could be given a short description of a model search (shown in Figure 6.12) and asked to identify which actions represented which phase of a search and why the searcher chose them. After a full group discussion of one case, the class could be split into smaller groups to look at multiple examples of cases of different types and repeat the analysis with each.

During the next class session in which work on the paper is scheduled, the first step in the process (topic refinement) would be highlighted by the instructor with a brief introduction on ways

Fill in the search step:

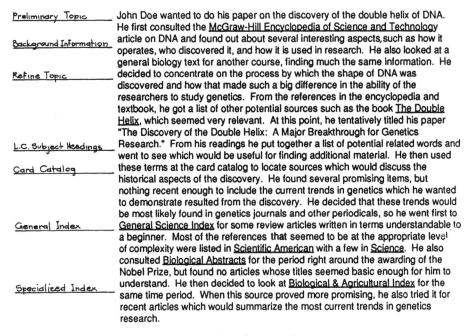

Preliminary Topic   John Doe wanted to do his paper on the discovery of the double helix of DNA.
He first consulted the McGraw-Hill Encyclopedia of Science and Technology
Background Information article on DNA and found out about several interesting aspects, such as how it
operates, who discovered it, and how it is used in research. He also looked at a
general biology text for another course, finding much the same information. He
Refine Topic   decided to concentrate on the process by which the shape of DNA was
discovered and how that made such a big difference in the ability of the
researchers to study genetics. From the references in the encyclopedia and
textbook, he got a list of other potential sources such as the book The Double
Helix, which seemed very relevant. At this point, he tentatively titled his paper
"The Discovery of the Double Helix: A Major Breakthrough for Genetics
L.C. Subject Headings Research." From his readings he put together a list of potential related words and
went to see which would be useful for finding additional material. He then used
Card Catalog   these terms at the card catalog to locate sources which would discuss the
historical aspects of the discovery. He found several promising items, but
nothing recent enough to include the current trends in genetics which he wanted
to demonstrate resulted from the discovery. He decided that these trends would
be most likely found in genetics journals and other periodicals, so he went first to
General Index   General Science Index for some review articles written in terms understandable to
a beginner. Most of the references that seemed to be at the appropriate level
of complexity were listed in Scientific American with a few in Science. He also
consulted Biological Abstracts for the period right around the awarding of the
Nobel Prize, but found no articles whose titles seemed basic enough for him to
understand. He then decided to look at Biological & Agricultural Index for the
Specialized Index   same time period. When this source proved more promising, he also tried it for
recent articles which would summarize the most current trends in genetics
research.

Figure 6.12 Sample case study of a search.

of using background information to narrow a topic. Then in small
groups, students would practice the procedure by using a sample
encyclopedia article to formulate a workable topic. At this point,
they would be introduced to the concept of the personal search
journal. The instructor would then have the students spend some
time recording in their journals how they plan to begin this process with whatever topics they might be considering for their
papers. Their assignment for the next session on research papers
would be to execute these initial plans and keep a record in the
journal on how things went.

These short segments devoted to the production of the paper
could be scheduled for twenty to thirty minutes once a week or

every other week. This timing would help to emphasize the evo-
lutionary nature of researching and writing.

At each scheduled paper period, the librarian would return to
discuss the results of the search process as the students have experienced it thus far. Since they now have some experiences on
which to base their participation, we could have them reflect on a
set of questions provided by the librarian, using their journal entries to document their observations. The questions might be the
following: "What was the most useful source of information
you've come across so far and why?" or "Give an example of a
blind alley you've run into and why you initially thought that
source would be useful." If the class has been particularly responsive, the librarian might ask, "What was the biggest problem
you've run into thus far?" and then poll the class for common
problems. They could then be used to guide the course instructor
and the librarian toward the kind of help that would be useful. If
the class were more sophisticated, these problems could then become the focus for brainstorming solutions. The instructor and librarian could then review the next steps in the process, illustrate
them with more detailed case examples which the students would
analyze, and have the students plan the next phase of their own
search by writing some of their ideas in their journals.

This cycle of review of research steps (explaining), case studies and journal entries (applying), "field work" in the library (experiencing), and class discussion and journal entries (examining)
could be reiterated several times during the semester, without the
need for the librarian's presence. The instructor could conduct the
discussion and record any particularly difficult questions to be
checked out with the librarian later.

At the end of the semester, students would turn in the journals along with their papers so that the instructor and librarian

could use the information to determine where students were having problems. If, as implied earlier, there is a desire to actually have students develop evaluative skills about searching, the journals from previous classes could be used as case studies in subsequent classes. Students could be asked to read the description of the search strategy and critique the decisions made at various points. Such a task would be more appropriate for more advanced students.

Step Six: Checking for Continuity with Learning Principles

This particular instructional design has a lot of positive aspects when considered from the learning theory point of view. Let's begin with the idea of motivation. As noted earlier in the discussion, these students should be well-motivated to engage in this learning. First, the library instruction is closely tied to their needs: the requirement to do a research paper for the class. Second, throughout the learning process, the students are given an opportunity to apply the principles being learned to their own specific situation through the use of the personal search journal and time spent in class on preparing materials for that journal. Finally, the instructor has enough personal stake in having students learn research skills that she gives it a regular time in class throughout the semester. This time commitment communicates to the students how important these concepts are and encourages students to make research a high priority as well. Adding to that message is the possibility that a large proportion of the instruction on these research skills could be done by the classroom instructor herself. She is someone who, by virtue of her position, carries a lot of influence with the students and should be able to motivate them to learn what is being offered, especially by linking it so closely with their already-required work.

From the standpoint of organization, the structure of the sequence described above has a lot to recommend it. To begin with, the instruction starts off with an overview of the steps of searching. This provides the organizational structure into which all subsequent steps will fit, thus making the learning easier. In addition, the larger process is broken down into smaller, easily digested pieces so that there is little danger of information overload in any one session. The smaller parts emphasize the step-by-step nature of the process. If we wanted to emphasize a more complex cognitive level than the basic step procedure, we would not divide the process up this way, but under these conditions the small chunks actually serve to accentuate the step-like nature of the procedure. Of course, both the course instructor and the librarian would be careful during any presentation to highlight these steps and provide new information in relation to its place in the overall procedure.

Perhaps the strongest aspect of the sequence of instruction is the emphasis on active responding. Learning does not proceed to the next step until the learners have had an opportunity to try out the previous step. The active responding is incorporated into the case studies used during class and into the planning portion of each class where the students write their intended out-of-class work in their journals. Since these first planning steps are usually the hardest in any task, the fact that they can be completed in class encourages the students to carry them out once they are out of class.

At the same time, of course, the inclusion of these activities during the class period allows the instructor to provide feedback about the accuracy of the students' understanding of the process before they go out to tackle the real library. This "practice" not only reinforces the learning but also prevents the students from being overly frustrated when they get to the actual library work. In this situation, feedback, the fourth learning concern, can come from the instructor during class, or the instructor may choose to

occasionally collect the journals and provide more extensive feedback by reading them outside of class.

The sequence of instruction planned for this class seems to
adequately cover all the four areas of learning which were discussed in Chapter 5. Added to that is the fact that the increased
opportunity for the librarian to get to know the students, should
she be the one to come to class when this instruction is being
done, may set the stage for even greater contact between the students and the library staff and contribute to some affective objectives which were not explicitly stated at the outset.

CASE FOUR

Perhaps the most familiar and frustrating teaching assignment
facing a librarian is the request from a well-meaning instructor to
"introduce my students to the library." This request was brought
to the library by an instructor in an introductory American history class of three hundred students. It didn't differ from a dozen
other similar requests.

This type of request is frustrating for most librarians because it is so vague. The instructor feels that the students should
know that the library is there as a very potent resource, and he is
interested in encouraging students to start their acquaintance with
it early in their college years. The size of this class, however, dis-
courages him from making an actual assignment for the students
to complete. The instructor who makes this type of request often
is unclear about exactly what students should know about the library other than a vague awareness of its existence. A second frustrating aspect of the request is the limitation on time. To do a
thorough job of "introducing students to the library" takes more
time than an instructor would be willing to give in a class like this.
The final frustration is that the students usually can't understand

why they're being subjected to this instruction and, therefore, are not as receptive to learning. And yet, it would be a shame to put any blocks in the path of this instructor, who at least recognizes that the students should know something about this wonderful resource. Some support of his request at this point could be leveraged into more significant inroads in future classes once he becomes convinced that the librarians are responsive. Therefore, the best tactic is to accept the challenge and work on modifying his request across semesters as trust is built.

Step One: The Objectives

As always, the librarian's first task should be to try to clarify the instructional objectives by talking to the instructor face-to-face about the course and how library services fit into it. Sometimes that process will help focus the required information sufficiently so the librarian can produce some reasonable objectives. In this type of situation, it may be useful to have a few potential objectives up your sleeve to suggest subtly along the way. Instructors are often at a loss when it comes to describing what they want, and a few careful suggestions will help them focus their own thinking. This also will increase your credibility as an expert in their eyes and smooth the path for getting at objectives you are interested in. After all, the librarian *is* the expert in this area; the instructor can't know as much as you do about recent developments in information services and library holdings.

In response to this overture by the librarian in this particular case, the instructor said that although he didn't intend to make any specific library assignments that semester, he wanted the students to know what a tremendous resource they had available to them and to encourage them to become comfortable with it because that's part of being a scholar.

Inherent in this statement are several concepts about the library that could serve as objectives for the instructional session. For example, the instructor mentioned what a tremendous *resource* the library is, so the librarian could focus on making the students aware of the unusual nature of a collegiate library in general and this one in particular and how it might be different from the libraries they're used to. Or the focus might be all the different things students could get from the library or do in the library besides just finding a book. The instructor also mentioned how a *scholar* uses the library. The librarian might be able to cooperate with the instructor to help the students understand how their professors use the library and how that compares with their own use of it.

Occasionally, the above strategy doesn't work and the librarian is left to interpret the phrase "introduction to the library"as he sees fit. The task is still one of defining some workable objectives. The one definite truth in this situation is that you cannot possibly convey to the students everything they need to know about using the library, so you must restrict yourself to four or five entry points which will at least get them started.

For example, one set of entry points might be different types of information that can be found in a library. The librarian might organize the objectives around the distinctions among books, periodicals, indexes, government documents, and audiovisual materials, and the reasons and procedures for accessing each type. Or the librarian might emphasize different uses which could be made of the library, such as researching a scholarly topic, planning a trip, finding entertaining reading, or figuring out how to accomplish some concrete task. Or the uses might be more narrowly focused to academic tasks which would highlight the major entry points into the library, such as locating a specific source, answering a specific question, getting general background reading, and so on.

To decide what entry points might be appropriate, we can invert the design process slightly and look at the students and course constraints for some hints about appropriate objectives. For example, if these students are new to post-secondary education in general, their immediate need would be to recognize how much is possible in a collegiate library as opposed to a public library or high-school library. If the students are brand new to the campus, they'll be struggling with the questions of how this system is organized, where things are, and what's available on this campus. If they have been at this campus for a while, the where and what of the library will not be as important as how to use it efficiently. If the course is a research-type course, then information about specialized materials on the subject would be best. If none of these is appropriate because the students don't even know what they need, you might base the objectives on the five most frequently asked questions that students bring to librarians.

So, for example, the following alternative sets of objectives might be appropriate for different groups:

Students new to higher education:	a) to list the possible uses of materials and services available in the library
	b) to list the differences in collection emphasis between college and other libraries
	c) to accept the library as a valuable resource
Students new to this campus:	a) to list the types of materials and services available from this library system
	b) to describe the four or five most common entry points into this library
	c) to accept the library as a valuable resource

Students familiar with *this campus*:	a) to make efficient use of the services available at this library b) to list the types of materials available in American history c) to accept the library as a valuable resource

Getting back to our sample class, the librarian has examined the students and decided to focus on two objectives based on what the instructor has said and the fact that these students are new to university life in general and this university in particular. The librarian has chosen as his objectives the following:

1) The students will be able to describe how the resources and procedures of a college library differ from a high-school or public library.

2) The students will be able to list at least five purposes of the library besides providing books for term papers.

3) The students will view the library as an approachable and valuable resource.

Whichever objectives are chosen in this situation, they are unlikely to be anything other than basic cognitive or affective objectives. There is no point in having objectives about the course content and the library jointly because there is nothing in the course's objectives about using the library for assignments and because the instructor has a more general goal in mind. Given these basic objectives, then, it is most likely that the librarian will be using some form of direct instruction.

Step Two: The Students

As noted earlier, the students in this case are probably new to the college environment, given the fact that this is an introductory-level course. They are unlikely to have much background in the content of the course or the library system. It would be particularly useful for a librarian faced with frequent requests of this type to become familiar with probable entry-level skills of incoming freshmen. By knowing how they are accustomed to using a library, the librarian can build on those skills, emphasizing similarities and differences. With students at this level, the librarian may be faced with helping them make a significant shift in the way they view potential use of the library. It is more than a question of amount of use; rather it is a whole new way of viewing the use. Getting the students to stop thinking of the library as a source of *books* and to start thinking of it as a source of *information* can be a formidable task, particularly if the librarian has forgotten how beginning users think about the library. By constantly reminding himself of those entry-level attitudes and skills, the librarian can be more sensitive to the problems of upgrading user sophistication.

The students in this course are also going to be fairly unsophisticated about learning skills in general. They will probably still be using the learning skills that were so successful in secondary school. They may also be at a fairly low cognitive level in terms of viewing the world. They may still be looking for "right" answers and, therefore, be unready to do much in the way of small-group activity or independent learning. The students' low level of learning skills plus their lack of sophistication in the content point toward direct instruction.

Step Three: The Situation

The biggest problem a librarian will face in this situation is a motivational one. The lack of any tie with course objectives means that students will be less than convinced of their need to know any of this stuff. The librarian will have to exploit as many of the means of enhancing motivation discussed in the previous chapter as possible. It will be important to be somewhat creative in the approach. The inclusion of humor and variety should be considered seriously. A straight recitation of facts would be deadly. For example, in a session using as its base the most frequently asked questions, the librarian might begin by displaying a list of humorous as well as serious questions.

The number of students also puts severe constraints on the choice of instruction. Large classes such as this one usually dictate more direct instruction. It is also likely that the classroom will be auditorium-like, given the class size, which makes group work and other forms of interactive learning more difficult. Therefore, any active learning will have to be done individually or in pairs and limited to strongly controlled activities focused on the presentation, such as answering quizzes or questionnaires along with the lecture.

The time constraints have already been mentioned. Their primary influence on the design will be to restrict the number of objectives which can be addressed in the class.

Step Four: The Instructor

Instructor skills needed in this situation are mostly presentation skills. The librarian must be lively enough to hold the attention of three hundred students for approximately fifty minutes. Since it is unlikely that the students will consider the content gripping enough to entrance them for the whole time, the librarian will have to depend on his own enthusiasm and personality to attract and hold their attention. Enthusiasm, variety, humor, and a responsiveness to the audience will be necessary components of this instruction. Because direct instruction is the likely choice in this situation, a great deal of attention will be focused on the instructor, who must be comfortable in that leadership role.

Constraint		Teaching Options
Objectives	Describe differences - Basic List uses of library - Basic View library as valuable - Affective	Direct Direct Indirect
Students	New to college Little background Entry-level learning skills	Direct
Situation	Large class Restrictive classroom Limited time Not much tie to class content	Direct but creative

Figure 6.13   Constraint analysis for Case Four.

Intermission: Taking Stock of Teaching Options

At this point, we can see in Figure 6.13 that all of our constraints seem to point to some form of direct instruction, with the exception of the affective objective, which would require indirect. In this case, the librarian is going to use a lecture method but try to get the students involved. Student involvement and the librarian's own enthusiasm will have to substitute for indirect instruction, given the other situational constraints.

Step Five: Sequencing Instruction

Let's consider how the librarian might use the learning cycle to sequence his lecture (Figure 6.14). First, he must assume some library exposure as the basis for experience in the experiencing phase. He begins by trying to draw on students' past library experiences and contrasting them with what the college library has to offer. To do this, he has made up a set of visuals contrasting what would be typical of a high-school or public library and what

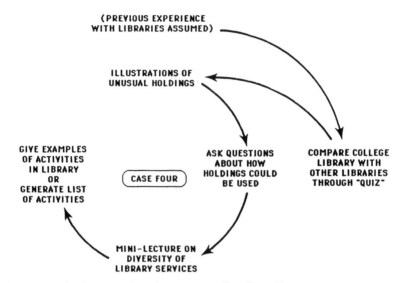

Figure 6.14 Instructional sequence for Case Four.

is typical of the college. He presents the information about the former and has the students guess on a sheet what they think the comparable information about the college's library is. For example, he might tell students the number of books in a typical high-school library and then ask them how many books they think the college has. After they've written down their answers, he tells them the correct number. Or he might first ask how many books they thought their high-school library contained and then give the average and contrast it with the college library. This comparison would be part of the examining phase of the cycle. Note that with three hundred students in the class, student involvement will be restricted to individual, private responses rather than general discussion. Only a few students will actually be asked to respond out loud. While this is not as effective as having each student personally respond, it accomplishes the spirit of the task.

The librarian follows these questions with a series of visuals showing some of the unusual holdings of the library. These activities are intended to give the students some vicarious experience about the novel nature of the college library and cause them to think a bit about what it means to them as students. The latter could be prompted through questions about how they might use these holdings, asking students to give some examples. This activity would be a type of "examining."

Next, he might proceed to give an overview of the services available in the library by listing a series of usual and unusual things a student could do or find in the library and where they would be. The purpose of this part is to show the diversity of services rather than give a comprehensive overview. If such an overview is desired, it is best provided in printed format. This overview is a further expansion of the "explaining" of the library structure. The librarian might conclude the session by inviting students to brainstorm other things they might find in the library, in a form of "applying," although this activity could get raucous and silly; nevertheless, it might end the session on a positive note, especially if the librarian can handle it all with a sense of humor. He will have accomplished his two cognitive objectives and an additional affective objective of portraying the library as a wonderful place to spend time. Finally, he should summarize the main themes he has chosen in a brief conclusion.

Step Six: Checking for Continuity with Learning Principles

Finally, of course, we want to know how well such a plan would tap our learning principles. Beginning with motivation, we noted that because the librarian couldn't depend on much course-based motivation, he would have to fall back on his own resources to motivate the students. The use of a question-guessing format for giving information has some motivation built into it. Most people like to get quiz answers right (witness the popularity of game shows on TV). By actively engaging the students in some guesses about comparisons between the systems that are familiar to them and this new system, the librarian may gain some motivation of that type. By pointing out novel or startling aspects of the library, he is tapping into the motivation value of novelty and curiosity. But most important will be the librarian's need to be personally dynamic, enthusiastic, and interesting.

Because the librarian will be using direct instruction, he will have no trouble providing a good solid organization to the material. His main task will be to select a few main themes on which to focus and to highlight those themes in the course of presenting the information. The use of visuals should help with this aspect of the task, but he should take care to organize his questions and facts around a few major themes and highlight those themes over and over.

Direct instruction usually doesn't provide much opportunity for active responding, but if the librarian uses the questions and brainstorming at the appropriate points in the sequence, he will have given some chance for responding and feedback. The feedback will be vicarious in that the students will have to compare their chosen responses to those made by other students or given by the librarian. While this design doesn't allow much in the way of active responding, the situation and student constraints are too difficult to overcome in this case. The librarian must be satisfied with what he can get.

CASE FIVE

Occasionally the instructional situations librarians deal with come not at the instigation of an instructor but through their own observations of student behavior in the library. In this case, the librarians in the Engineering Library noticed that every semester thirty-five to eighty students were coming in at the same time to find material needed to write a specification. Since most engineering students have had little experience with the holdings of the library outside of assignments in their liberal arts courses, the librarians were spending a lot of hours on individual help for students. After several semesters of this pattern, the librarians decided to approach the instructor to discuss a more organized way of handling this bulge in the work load. They hoped to make more efficient use of their own time as well as that of these very time-conscious students.

The head librarian contacted the instructor of the course "Construction Standards and Specifications" to get some information about the course and how they could work together to make the students' use of the library more efficient. The librarian discovered that the course was a junior-level course in civil engineering required for both civil and architectural engineering students. Each semester one or two sections were taught, each having from thirty-five to forty students.

The assignment with which the students were struggling was one of the major requirements of the class. In it, the students had to write a construction specification on a project of their choice, such as a driveway, roofing system, foundation, or moisture barrier. The assignment involved finding out how the particular type of construction was done, determining what the government and industry standards were, and then locating products that would comply with those standards. In order to pass the course, the students had to complete this assignment satisfactorily. They received little guidance from the instructor and had about a week and a half to finish. It was no wonder they seemed so harried.

Step One: The Objectives

One advantage of working with many technical courses is that the objectives of their assignments are usually fairly clear and the instructors are accustomed to working with specifications, which is what objectives are in the broader sense. The assignment with which the students were grappling had several technical objectives about the solution of construction problems and the communication of construction specifications to the builder. The library objectives were a subcomponent of the assignment. Of course, the instructor had not specifically included objectives for the library work, but they were easily deduced from the requirements. The library objectives were the following:

1) Given a list of sources on various construction processes, the students will be able to find one that describes how to build their chosen project.
2) Students will be able to locate government and industry standards and specifications that pertain to their project.
3) Students will be able to use the product catalogs to identify products that meet the standards.

All three of these are intermediate cognitive objectives involving the use of sources to answer a specific need. Implicit in all are the knowledge of which sources exist, a basic cognitive objective. However, as in our earlier example, it is probably not necessary for these students to know the specific sources as long as they know that alternatives are available and how to use them. The knowledge that the sources exist as a basic cognitive objective implies a direct instruction mode, while the ability to use the sources implies semi-direct instruction.

Step Two: The Students

These students present an interesting problem for the librarians. They are highly motivated to accomplish this task but have some characteristics that will be important to consider in choosing instruction. First, like most technically-oriented students, engineering students have a heavy schedule of required courses and very little time. They prize very highly anything that can save them a lot of time. This is a motivation that can be used to convince them to put in a little time learning about what the librarians have to offer. Second, technically-oriented students also tend to prefer fairly clear-cut, step-by-step procedure descriptions similar to the problems they are accustomed to solving. They don't tolerate ambiguity well but prefer things that can be categorized and listed neatly. Third, engineering students, while sophisticated learners, are not usually very familiar with library use because most technically-oriented courses do not require it. Library use with which they are familiar will be that from their liberal arts courses or high-school background. Many of the skills appropriate for library work in those settings would not be as useful in the technical fields and could actually interfere with efficient use of the technical literature.

Fortunately for the librarians in this case, however, is the powerful motivation of the course assignment. Not only must the students pass this assignment in order to pass the course—a definite motivator—but they will be working on an assignment that is very closely related to what they will be doing as professionals, and therefore, it has a lot of face validity (i.e., it looks reasonable).

On the whole, the student constraints in this case would cause us to lean toward semi-direct instruction, since the learners are sophisticated enough about following procedures to benefit from and feel comfortable with this type of learning. There will be some need for direct instruction in those areas where background in the content is insufficient to allow them to get started without a little help.

Step Three: The Situation

There are several constraining factors in this case. In the first place, the instructor has no interest in giving over any class time to anything other than engineering, a typical response in heavily technical courses. There are, unfortunately, too many students to make individual one-to-one tutoring efficient, which was the reason the librarians raised the issue in the first place. A further complication is that the materials the students need to use are primarily microforms, which must be used in the library and are in heavy use by other students. Therefore, the instruction must be flexible enough to occur when the students have an opportunity to use the equipment rather than monopolizing the equipment for instruction to the detriment of other students. Also, given the limited time the instructor has allowed for the completion of the assignment and the number of students who need to use the materials, it would be best to allow the instruction to occur whenever the students need it and can get access to the equipment. All these factors would cause us to lean toward individual rather than group instruction for most of the learning.

Step Four: The Instructor

Since we are leaning toward individual instruction, the instructor skills that will be of most use in this case are those required in the preparation of stand-alone materials. There are organizational and analytical skills that would enable the librarians to determine just what the major steps in the process should be and to clearly mark them for the students. The librarians should also be able to anticipate where students will have problems and make provisions to have extra guidance at those points in the sequence. This often means preparing the materials sufficiently in advance of their use so that they can be pilot-tested on a sample group of users and any problems can be corrected before classes begin using them.

Constraint		Teaching Options
Objectives	Choose source - Intermediate	Semi-direct
	Locate standards - Intermediate	Semi-direct
	Use product catalogs - Intermediate	Semi-direct
	Know which sources exist - Basic	Direct
Students	Highly motivated	
	Some background in library, but limited to a different area	Semi-direct
	Prefer clear-cut steps	
Situation	Large number of students	
	No class time	Individual
	Resources only available in library	

Figure 6.15   Constraint analysis for Case Five.

Intermission: Taking Stock of Teaching Options

As Figure 6.15 indicates, the two driving forces in this case are the objectives and the situational constraints. The objectives indicate the need for some direct instruction to provide information about the types of sources available, plus semi-direct instruction to guide the students through the steps of using the materials. The situational constraints require that this instruction be done on an individual rather than group basis. Therefore, the combination of these two factors leads us to choose printed materials as the basic direct instruction which will provide the information about the sources and a workbook with step-by-step instructions on using the sources. The printed materials would list and describe the various construction handbooks available in the library; the workbook would use the sequence of a model example for each step and the provision of space at each step for the students to follow that model while using their own topic. There might also be a need for

point-of-use guides where the standards and specifications, product catalogs, and microform reader/printers are located. The semi-
direct instruction would thus teach both how to use the sources
(e.g., how to look up a product) and how to apply what the source
offers to a particular topic (e.g., how information on specifications
fits into the construction plan).

Step Five: Sequencing Instruction

In this case, the learning cycle is primarily useful in designing the
workbook sequence rather than the overall instructional sequence.
In this instance, because the students have no background experience on which to draw, the cycle (Figure 6.16) would begin at the
explaining phase by describing how a particular source is used. The
students would then follow that model in the applying phase by
attempting to carry out the steps with an example, after which
that attempt could be compared with the correct answer to en-

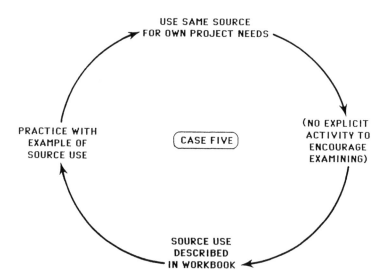

Figure 6.16 Instructional sequence for Case Five.

sure understanding. Then in the experiencing phase, the students would attempt to use that same procedure with their own project. As with many cycles that start at "explaining," there would be no opportunity to "examine" other than reflecting on the ease with which the model steps were applied to the students' own project.

The entire learning sequence would be initiated by the instructor of the course who would distribute the workbooks. The workbook itself would incorporate the step-by-step process required to identify appropriate sources and use those sources in solving the specification problems. Each source would have a point-of-use guide to assist students in locating information in it. Completion of the workbook would then form the basis for the students' construction specifications. The workbook could be turned in along with the assignment to document the students' work, or the instructor may allow the students to retain the workbook for future use. If the workbooks are submitted, they can provide the librarians with valuable information about the ease with which the students were able to complete the projects and use the materials in the library.

Step Six: Checking for Continuity with Learning Principles

As noted earlier, there should be a lot of inherent motivation in this assignment, since it should enable students to complete their construction specifications more easily. The librarians should take care that this relationship is clear to the students in the format and final version of the workbook. Making the end product of completing the workbook conform to the instructor's specifications can go a long way toward enhancing student motivation for completing it. The closer the workbook conforms to their professional needs, the more it will be perceived as valuable. The fact that this instruction is designed to be done at the student's convenience is another source of motivation. Most students will work better when allowed to choose the time of the instruction. Also, the fact that feedback is built into the workbook so that the students can see that they are making progress should be a source of motivation as well. Finally, if the librarians can convince the instructor to give this exercise his stamp of approval, the students will be even more convinced of its value.

The organization of the learning will be provided by the models used in the workbook. The step-by-step nature of the task should make the organization fairly apparent.

Implicit in the notion of a workbook are the active responding and feedback requirements of learning. The students will be working through examples and immediately applying them to their own project. The only danger is that some students will be tempted to skip over the actual examples and believe that simply reading the descriptions is sufficient. There is not a lot the librarians can do about this, but the course instructor can require the working through of examples as part of the assignment if he is convinced of their value. The examples are, at least, built into the instruction and will enhance any presentation of content, provided they are used.

One final advantage of this particular instructional method has nothing to do with the instruction itself. Rather it is the fact that time spent on the production of workbooks of this type will pay off for the librarians with repeated semesters of use. The workbooks allow the students to work at their own pace, while allowing the librarians to concentrate their time on those students who need extra help. This is an all-around good use of everyone's time.

CASE SIX

Since joining the reference staff of a large university library system, the business reference librarian has been inundated with requests from faculty for library instruction sessions on a variety of business-related assignments that have one thing in common: They are all dependent on the use of company and industry information sources. The courses involved, which are offered from management, finance, and business communications departments, to name a few, range from sophomore to graduate levels. The number of students enrolled in each course varies, as does the sophistication level of the students. The librarian has come to realize, though, that most business students, regardless of the level of the course, are unfamiliar with the sources needed to do the assignments they are getting.

After several semesters of spending inordinate amounts of time preparing for each separate class, the librarian realizes that she must do something to manage these demands on her time more efficiently. What she needs is an instructional sequence or set of materials that will cover the company/industry sources, but remain flexible enough to meet the assignment needs of the students in the different courses. While this is slightly different from designing instruction for a particular setting, it is a useful concept to keep in mind when one receives many similar requests in a semester or across semesters.

Step One: The Objectives

In preparation for her task, the librarian reviews the copies of the assignments she has dealt with in the past, trying to determine if there are any commonalities in the instructors' objectives. This review reveals essentially the same objective for most classes, which is sometimes stated but usually implied: "Students will use the

library to find information about companies and industries." It is
what the students do with this information once they find it that
varies from course to course. In some classes, they are preparing
prospectuses for investment purposes; in others they research companies for employment opportunities; in still others, the information is used for market research or product development. Regardless of the end use, the initial task is the same: to find facts about
specific companies or industries.

With this information in hand, the librarian restates the general objective in more specific terms:

1)   Students will be able to list the sources available on com-
     panies and industries.
2)   Students will be able to describe the types of sources and
     kinds of information to be found in each type.
3)   Students will be able to select the sources needed for their
     particular assignment.
4)   Students will be able to plan an efficient search strategy.

The first two objectives are basic cognitive objectives requiring
only the knowledge of what exists. The third is an intermediate objective requiring the student to apply the knowledge of sources to
a given problem. The fourth is an advanced objective as implied
in the word "efficient" because that requires planning and judg-
ment. It is these last two objectives that will vary the most from
class to class, although some aspect of each will probably be present in most classes.

Step Two: The Students

Assessing student characteristics in a situation like this is similar
to the problems the librarians faced in designing instruction for
the on-line catalog; the learners themselves are somewhat faceless
except for some very general characteristics. They will have widely

varying backgrounds in their familiarity with the business literature because many different classes must be serviced. The same is
true for their familiarity with the library at this university; the
levels of classes for which the materials are intended range from
sophomores who would know little about the given library to
graduate students who should be very familiar with it. On the
other hand, because they are all college students, they will have
some familiarity with libraries in general and some modest claim
to learning skills, though the latter would also vary quite a bit.
All we can be sure of is that they are not totally inept learners.

Although the students who will eventually use these materials will vary in their level of sophistication of content and
learning, as we have seen, they do share a high level of motivation. Business students at this librarian's campus, for the most
part, are a very competitive group. And for most of the classes
in question, the use of library sources is an integral part of their
course work, necessary to allow them to accomplish some assignment, rather than an exercise in a vacuum. Therefore, the librarian can count on their wanting to master these objectives to some
extent.

Step Three: The Situation

Since the materials are intended to be useful in a wide range of
courses, they should be designed to be independent of the class
situation; they should be useful regardless of the situation. About
the only constraint that some librarians would have to confront
in this faceless situation is a problem with reproduction of materials. Since there is no way to predict how many copies of any
materials the librarian might have to provide, it would be wise to
make the materials as compact as possible so that reproduction
costs and bulk do not defeat their usefulness in large classes. Also,
in anticipation of having to use the materials with large classes, the

librarian should attend to any physical details that will make their use easier to communicate to such groups. For example, color coding the pages or using distinctive markings for headings is preferable to having to refer to a given page number. Most students deal more easily with flipping to the "pink" section than turning to page 23.

Step Four: The Instructor

To be maximally useful, the materials should not depend on instructor skills for success. It should be possible for instructors of any bent to find something useful in them. On the other hand, the librarian designing these materials will need several skills. She will need to be able to organize the content in modules so that later she or another can choose which parts need to be included in a given situation. She will also need to be able to anticipate a variety of uses and find a common denominator around which to build the materials so they can be used readily in any of those situations, both from a conceptual standpoint and from a physical standpoint.

Intermission: Taking Stock of Teaching Options

At this point, we don't have much to go on in terms of instructional design except for the objectives. All other constraints are open and yet need to be considered. The objectives are a combination of basic, intermediate, and advanced skills. The basic skills call for direct instruction, the intermediate for semi-direct, and the advanced for indirect methods, normally. Since we can't predict the setting in which the materials will be used, we might assume that if we use an individual design, we will develop materials that could be used in any setting. So, for example, choosing an individual direct method such as printed materials for the first two objectives, an individual semi-direct method such as a workbook for the third objective, and a computer simulation of some sort for the fourth objective, the bases for each of these could be adapted to group methods as well, should the opportunity be available.

Given these constraints, the librarian decides to focus on the first two objectives (they could be covered with the same method regardless of situational constraints or student differences) and develop a printed handout that lists and describes the major sources of corporate and industry information.

If the facilities are available to her, the librarian might even be able to have this information accessible in a computer data base format, which would facilitate updating and would allow her to print out a master copy of a handout organized according to the needs of a particular course. The data base would contain all the information on each source, but would be coded with all the appropriate categories for type of information available. Then, if the course in question focuses primarily on fiscal data, the data base could be sorted according to types of fiscal information available. If the course was primarily one on marketing, the data base could be sorted according to types of marketing information. Thus the librarian could custom-make the handout for a given class without very much effort.

The business librarian envisions using these handouts in many ways. For example, she could distribute them to support a team-member teaching exercise, in which each student would learn about a particular source and then teach the others in the group about it. She could use the materials to supplement a simulation that focuses on selecting sources or a case study approach that illustrates search strategy techniques. These would be consistent with the third and fourth objectives. Or she could design a supplementary worksheet that would take students through the steps of the search strategy and give them space to record their findings, which would satisfy those objectives as well.

In addition to their usefulness in classroom settings, the handouts could be picked up by individual students who are not enrolled in the target courses but need the information. The handouts might be available at the reference desk to assist the librarians in individual work with students. If the computerized data base is a possibility, there might even be a workstation near the reference desk to allow for individual handouts to be printed on demand.

The beauty of this scheme is that the librarian's time is put to fairly efficient use in the production of the initial handout or the data base. Once that task is done, it is simply a matter of selecting the appropriate sort for the class in question.

Steps Five and Six: Sequencing Instruction and Checking for Continuity with Learning Principles

Since there is no actual instruction involved in the development of these multi-use materials, there is no need to concern ourselves with the sequencing of the instruction or conforming with learning principles. These concerns only enter into the librarian's plans as she begins to actually use the materials in a class setting.

CASE SEVEN

The instructor in a graduate research methods course in nutrition comes into the library to talk to someone about her plans for her course this semester. She is new to campus and is anxious to meet some of the library staff; she has worked with librarians at her previous institution. The instructor hands the chemistry librarian an assignment sheet that describes the course's research project: Students will define a research problem they will investigate in their dissertation, conduct a literature review to learn what has been done previously concerning the problem, and propose a research study they will conduct and report on in their dissertation.

After a few minutes of discussion, the librarian and instructor concentrate on the literature review. The librarian points out that the library has just acquired BRS AFTER DARK, which is being offered free of charge to all students and faculty. He is anxious to incorporate this source into the professor's request. On her part, the professor confesses that this is a service with which she is totally unfamiliar; it was not available at her previous institution. She is pleased to learn of this new tool, both for her students and for her own sake.

Step One: The Objectives

Based on the instructor's statement and their discussion, the librarian derives the following objective for the library part of the assignment:

> Students will be able to perform a data base search to review the literature on their dissertation topics.

Sub-objectives are the following:

1) Students will be able to describe the advantages of on-line searching (basic cognitive).
2) Students will be able to identify key concepts in their statement of the topic to be searched (intermediate cognitive).
3) Students will be able to list possible synonyms for each concept in a search, using truncation as necessary (intermediate cognitive).
4) Students will be able to use boolean operators to group concepts and form a search statement (basic and intermediate cognitive).

5)   Given a brief description of available data bases, students will be able to choose those that are appropriate for the topic and explain their reasons for their choice (advanced cognitive).

6)   Students will be able to use the computer terminal and execute the search as planned (intermediate cognitive).

7)   Students will be able to use search results to refine their search statement and plan the next steps of their search (advanced cognitive).

Step Two: The Students

As graduate students, the group is sophisticated in learning and in using the library, although they have probably had little or no experience with on-line searching in general and especially with BRS AFTER DARK because it is new to the campus. They are reasonably motivated because the research they perform in this class will be used in their dissertations. In addition, their motivation will be greatly increased when they find out they will be using the computer. Because graduate students are perpetually concerned about time and how little they have, anything that can save time is usually of great interest to them, particularly with regard to what they perceive as the more tedious aspects of their dissertations, including comprehensive literature searches. An additional source of motivation is the model of the professer herself, who has displayed openness to keeping up-to-date on the latest tools in her field.

Step Three: The Situation

Because this is a small class—only twenty students—almost any instructional method could be used. It would even be possible to bring the students to the library for instruction and reschedule the class to another time slot for one session. This is a frequent practice with graduate classes of this type.

One problem the librarian initially encountered with the instructor was her reluctance to devote more than one three-hour class period to this topic. During their discussions, however, the librarian appropriately pointed out that the number and complexity of the objectives to be taught called for exposure over a period of time rather than trying to include everything in one session; it would probably be counterproductive to devote an entire three-hour session to these objectives. It seemed a better model to spread exposure to these objectives over two or three sessions, each time devoting only part of a class period to library research skills. This strategy would have the added psychological advantage of not appearing to set these objectives apart from the general content of the course. Rather, they would be viewed as part of the orderly process of preparing a research proposal, which would be a better model for the students. As a result of this discussion, the nutrition instructor formulates a plan to devote portions of her class every other week to various aspects of preparing a research proposal, which is in line with the overall objective of the course as a whole, and to incorporate the instruction in library skills as part of that component of the course rather than as a separate component.

Step Four: The Instructor

In this situation, the level of the class and the course instructor's plan require not so much in the way of teaching skills from the librarian, but more in the area of professional competence and confidence. As instructors begin to work with graduate students and faculty peers, they shed the mantle of "teacher" and assume that of "professional consultant." This is a change in role and self-concept which requires a different set of skills more in line with those required by indirect instruction. For this situation, the librarian is going to be a facilitator and expert who helps the learners choose what is best for them. This will require a very good grasp of the possibilities and an ability to adapt to the needs of the learners. It will also require a willingness to allow the learners to be in control of what is learned to a great extent, which may be the hardest task of all.

The teaching skills that will be needed will be primarily in terms of being able to give brief, clear explanations and respond to questions as the learners pursue their own directions. Some of the middle objectives may call for question-asking skills and exercise-design skills as well.

Intermission: Taking Stock of Teaching Options

At this point, the two most influential constraints on our choice of methods are the objectives and the learners. As Figure 6.17 indicates, the objectives tend to be intermediate to advanced cognitive, which imply semi-direct to indirect methods of instruction. The learners, being more sophisticated and self-directed than in our previous cases, also lean us toward semi-direct and indirect instruction in most cases. Only the basic information about on-line searching and boolean operators is appropriate for some direct instruction. Fortunately, the situational constraints are minimal or can be worked out with the course instructor.

Step Five: Sequencing Instruction

Let's look at Figure 6.18 to see how these sessions would be sequenced. During his first visit to the class, the librarian's goal is to illustrate the advantages of on-line searching and bring the students to the point of having a search statement and data base selection. He begins by assuming that all of the students have some previous experience with manual searches that he can draw on as the experiencing phase of the learning cycle. For the examining

Constraint		Teaching Options
Objectives	Describe advantages - Basic	Direct
	Identify key concepts - Intermediate	Semi-direct
	List synonyms - Intermediate	Semi-direct
	Use boolean logic - Basic and intermediate	Direct and semi-direct
	Choose data bases - Advanced	Indirect
	Use terminal and execute search - Intermediate	Semi-direct
	Refine search statement - Advanced	Indirect
Students	Graduate students	
	Sophisticated learners	
	Familiar with library but not on-line or BRS After Dark	Semi-direct or indirect
	Highly motivated	
Situation	Small class	
	No time limits	Anything
	No class restrictions	

Figure 6.17 Constraint analysis for Case Seven.

phase, he asks them to recall their experiences and, specifically, how they went about such searches and the problems they encountered. He then uses these anecdotes to compare with the procedures of on-line searching, pointing out the advantages of the latter procedure, especially in terms of saving time and comprehensiveness. He also brings out drawbacks of the procedure with some suggestions about how they might be overcome. This is done with a mini-lecture/discussion format and should accomplish the first objective.

Next the librarian uses a demonstration/performance format to illustrate how to prepare for going on-line, covering objectives two through five. The students are given a worksheet which takes them through each step. The demonstration is interrupted after

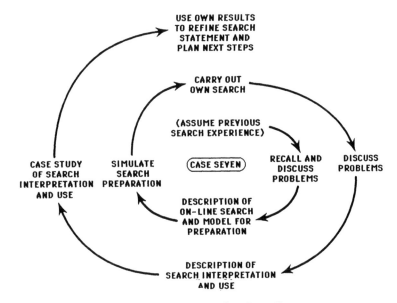

Figure 6.18 Instructional sequence for Case Seven.

each step with a short practice example to be done on the work-sheet. These demonstrations are part of the explaining phase.

Once all the preparation steps have been demonstrated and practiced, the librarian divides the class into five small groups and has them go through the process with a given topic, simulating what they would have to do before going on-line. Each group ends up with a search statement and data base selection. This exercise is the first of the applying phases. These results are discussed by the class as a whole, emphasizing that different search statements can be written for one topic. Each student then receives a blank worksheet to prepare for his or her own real search. The session ends with directions from the course instructor for students to prepare and conduct a search on their own topic sometime during the next three weeks. The librarian indicates that when the students have completed the worksheet and are ready for a search, the library staff would be available to review the worksheets before the students actually go on-line.

The librarian also points out that BRS AFTER DARK is a menu-driven system with automatic log-on procedures; instruction in executing the search is available at the terminals. He had previously decided that these learners were sophisticated enough to be able to handle this phase of their learning independently, and class time needed to be devoted to the more difficult cognitive aspects of this task. The point-of-use instruction made available could be similar to the on-line catalog instruction described in Case Two or could be in the form of printed instructions; either option would run through a sample search and clearly differentiate the system's prompts from the information the user must enter. (Note that this segment of instruction is not part of the illustrated Kolb cycle.)

During the next class session devoted to this activity, the librarian conducts a discussion during which he encourages students to indicate problems, questions, and reactions they had to their attempt to do a search. This discussion would be the examining phase of the cycle. During this time he tries to deal with problems they have mentioned more than once and reiterate that part of the previous class's discussion that might deal with these problems.

Since each student has come to class with a printout of search results, the librarian now begins the second round of the cycle, which will focus on interpreting and using the printout. He provides a handout that indicates how to read search results and leads a discussion on how to use these results to modify the search statement and continue with the research process. He also mentions the availability of paid searches that are executed by librarians. The librarian then distributes sample output from a fictional student's search and that student's plans for the next steps; the small groups work through this case study in a second application phase. Each student then spends some time with his or her own printout, replicating the process just gone through by the group in the final experience phase.

Step Six: Checking for Continuity with Learning Principles

The librarian was fortunate in this case to be working with a group which was already highly motivated to learn what he had to offer. Just to reinforce that motivation, he incorporated some fairly obvious reminders of the source of that motivation. By beginning with a discussion of the problems of manual searching, the librarian can highlight for the learners the advantages of on-line searching, just in case they were not already obvious. He also worked with the instructor to make the learning of these skills an integral part of the course rather than a separate concept. This allowed the weight of the course motivation to enhance the learning of the library skills. Through the exercises and timing of the instruction, he also tied the skills to be learned to the actual individual interests of the students, always ending each cycle with the application of the principles to the students' own work. This not only highlighted the relevance of what was being learned but also tapped the inherent interest each student already had for the topic which he or she chose to work on. Finally, the librarian allowed some of the instruction to be done on the students' own initiative (the actual on-line searching), thus giving them the feeling of control over their own learning, another source of motivation.

By breaking the instruction into two parts, the librarian is able to focus on the critical skills involved in each part separately, so that each can get the attention it deserves independently. The alternating between demonstration of a step and its execution by the learners also helps to reinforce the step-by-step nature of the task and contributes to its organizational structure. The use of the worksheet format also enhances that organization.

It is likely that the discussion about interpreting and using the printout will not be as organized as the description of how to prepare for a search. The librarian will have to take care to impose some organization on this phase of the instruction by incorporating an overview and a summary of what went on in the discussion. The emphasis on the individual student's needs will make organization of this phase more difficult.

Since most of the instruction will be in the demonstration/ performance, simulation, or case study format, there is ample opportunity for active responding. The only caution will be that the librarian will have to be sure to allow the students' needs to direct the course of these exercises. These more sophisticated learners resist having their responses directed too much.

The provision for lots of active responding also means the opportunity for lots of feedback. Here the librarian is indeed fortunate because the sophistication level of these learners means that they can easily provide feedback to one another. It will not fall on the librarian's shoulders to respond to everything. All he needs to remember is to permit the students to do just that by allowing them to work in groups at several stages of the instruction.

On the whole, this instructional sequence conforms fairly well to the principles of learning and should be successful.

CASE EIGHT

The English department in a large public university is in the midst of changing their curriculum to require a research paper in their freshman writing class, and the library staff hears about it through the grapevine. Because of the number of students involved and because of the rare opportunity to provide library instruction for the entire freshman class, the staff recognizes the need to be involved while the new requirement is still in the planning stages. After a brief meeting with the department head to obtain a copy of the new library assignment and to discuss their participation in it, the librarians meet to outline an instructional sequence which they will present to the English department's curriculum committee.

Step One: The Objectives

The English department's implied objective for the research paper assignment is the following: Students will be able to write an informative paper which is a synthesis of materials found in the library. This overall objective contains both composition and library skills objectives, and the librarians begin the design process by focusing on the latter. The students enrolled in freshman English are new to campus, so the library objectives will have to cover both orientation to the library and instruction in research skills. The orientation component includes the following:

1) Students will be able to locate the essential areas in the library (reference, reserve, and circulation desks; card catalog; reference collection; serials list; periodicals section; stacks; audiovisual collection).

2) Students will be able to follow the procedures for finding and borrowing books, locating periodicals, and using the reserve collection.

The first is a basic cognitive objective; the second is an intermediate cognitive objective involving application procedures, with the implied basic objective of knowing what the procedures are. The librarians decide to furnish this basic information and look for a way to give students the opportunity to apply the procedures in the course of the orientation.

The research skills component includes the following objectives:

1) Students will be able to follow a search strategy that will lead to finding information in a logical progression from background materials to recent developments.
2) Students will be able to find an overview of a topic in appropriate background sources and use that information to narrow the topic;
3) Students will be able to find books on a topic by using the *Library of Congress Subject Headings*, subject catalog, and location chart.
4) Students will be able to find articles on a topic using both general and specialized periodical indexes and the serials list.

All of these are intermediate cognitive objectives (applying specific skills to a given situation), with knowledge of both the search strategy process and the available sources implied. Given the level of students, the librarians decide to furnish this basic information and focus instruction on implementing a prescribed search strategy and choosing from a list of potential sources. As the students become more familiar with their chosen fields of study, they will need to be able to plan a search strategy and list and describe particular sources as those most appropriate to their needs.

In addition to the above objectives, the librarians are interested in encouraging the course instructors to include one more type of objective: some of the affective objectives which are seldom dealt with and yet are the source of a lot of problems for instructors and librarians. For example, many course instructors are concerned about the problems of plagiarism and improper use of sources; librarians are upset with the increasing mutilation and theft of library materials. As part of the objectives for this course, objectives dealing with these two issues are included. For the librarians' concerns, the following objective is constructed:

> Students will follow library regulations on the care of materials.

Step Two: The Students

Although students come to the university with varying levels of skill in using the library, depending on what was available in their high schools, they are all basically uninitiated in the use of a collection of this size and complexity, and they are unfamiliar with most of the resources that will be covered in the library unit. As freshmen, they are also fairly unsophisticated learners, accustomed to more supervision from their high-school instructors than they are likely to get at the university.

An additional complicating factor is that while they are somewhat motivated because the instruction will be tied in to their assignment, many students think they know a great deal more about using the library than they actually do (the "I-learned-all-about-that-in-high-school" syndrome).

Step Three: The Situation

The number of students who must be taught is probably the overriding factor in this case. The English department typically schedules over 50 sections of the course each semester, with 25 students in each section, for a total of 1,250 students a semester. Even if the librarians did nothing more than visit each class once during the semester to "introduce" them to the library, the task would be impossible, since the number of sections is so large and all would need their instruction at about the same time of the semes-

ter. And bringing each section to the library for a tour would
seriously disrupt the work of the other students using the facilities.

Complicating matters is the fact that a large number of objectives has been planned for the library unit, and this number
would require more time than a single class session. Therefore,
this would increase the number of hours the librarians would
have to devote to just this one course, to the detriment of all the
other library services. In addition, each course instructor has control over how much time the library unit is given for his or her
class, thus requiring the unit to be flexible enough to meet the
varying amounts of time allotted.

Since the librarians are also trying to instill in the students
the cumulative nature of the literature search process, they would
like to spread the instruction over a period of several weeks. Con-
vincing all the freshman composition instructors of the need for
this is a difficult task.

Step Four: The Instructor

Given the constraints on librarian time dictated by the situation,
the librarians are forced to rely on the classroom instructors to
oversee the library instruction unit. This means that instructor
qualities are going to be quite variable and are not to be depended
upon. The instruction must be fairly independent of instructor
skills if it is to be uniform across the sections. The objectives that
are likely to get fairly widespread instructor acceptance are those
that deal with attitude, including plagiarism and proper use of library materials. Most instructors will probably be willing to work
hard on achieving those objectives. About all the librarians can do
concerning instructor skills for the other objectives is to make the
material appear so relevant that the instructors will recognize the

Constraint		Teaching Options
Objectives	Locate areas - Basic	Direct
	Follow procedures - Intermediate	Semi-direct
	Follow strategy - Intermediate	Semi-direct
	Narrow topic - Intermediate	Semi-direct
	Use subject headings and card catalog - Intermediate	Semi-direct
	Use indexes - Intermediate	Semi-direct
	Subscribe to library rules - Affective	Semi-direct or indirect
Students	Little background in research library Unsophisticated learners	Direct or semi-direct
Situation	Large number of students Large number of objectives No control of in-class time	Individual or direct group

Figure 6.19 Constraint analysis for Case Eight.

importance of the unit and want to give it their best. After that, there is not much the librarians can do about the instructors.

Intermission: Taking Stock of Teaching Options

At this point, as Figure 6.19 indicates, the dominant considerations in the instructional design appear to be the number of students who must be served and the inability of the library staff to handle all their needs. Because the library staff can't do the instruction in groups, they must produce individual instruction formats which will meet the same objectives or depend on the classroom instructor to do the instruction in library skills. Since the latter is an uncertain quantity, the librarians choose to use more individual methods for most of the instruction and group methods only where nothing else will do and the course instructor has some stake in the outcome.

The librarians decide to cover the orientation objectives in a self-guided tour/exercise and the research skills component in a workbook, both semi-direct formats. The materials would represent the basis of a library instructional unit which the instructor would incorporate into the class activities as he or she deemed appropriate.

The self-guided tour would include an exercise with multiple-choice questions that require students to go to each of the key areas in the library and also use each of the tools that will help them locate the sources they will need in the research component (card catalog, serials list, location chart). The workbook would allow the students to research topics of their choice rather than assigned topics, the approach typically used in workbooks. The materials would include a worksheet that outlines the steps of the search strategy, with room for students to record their findings, and a series of handouts that describe the types of sources students would use at each step of the process (background sources, books, periodical articles). To facilitate using the various handouts with the worksheet, the librarians plan to package them in three-ring binders. Unlike a workbook that requires students to examine all of the sources listed and answer questions about each source, students would select only those that pertain to their own topic. The library staff also outlines a series of signs to help students locate the stopping points on the tour and point-of-use aids to explain how to use the various tools covered in the handouts.

The printed materials would free librarians from in-class contact with students, something the library staff cannot handle with the number of students involved, and instead emphasize student-librarian interaction in the library when students need the most help. Librarians would act as resource people, supplementing and clarifying information in the printed materials and giving students feedback. By making the instructional materials available to students when they would be using library resources, the proposed methods would also place the instruction in the library, at the time and place of need.

One problem with using these semi-direct methods with what are essentially fairly unsophisticated learners is that they may have difficulty using them at first. The librarians will need to be sure that the first few steps in the process are small and easy to complete and that the course instructors monitor these early steps closely. As the students become more familiar with the materials and the library, the monitoring can taper off and the materials can become more complex. Nevertheless, it is in the early stages of use that students will need help from classroom instructors and librarians alike.

In using this approach, the librarians realize they are putting a lot of responsibility in the hands of the course's instructors, and some may not spend enough class time on library instruction. The workbook, therefore, must include enough instruction to make up for lack of in-class teaching by faculty. To help alleviate this problem, the librarians plan an information packet for the faculty that would include suggestions for introducing the library unit and the materials designed by the library staff, dealing with common student problems such as narrowing a topic, and conducting other in-class exercises to supplement the materials. The librarians also need to negotiate with the English department for time to meet with faculty to orient them to the new library assignment and this way of handling it.

For the affective objectives, the librarians plan to use an attitude clarification exercise as described in the section on synergogic methods (Chapter 3). The librarians create a questionnaire dealing with both academic issues such as plagiarism and library issues such as materials abuse. The course instructors could then use these materials to conduct the exercise and help the students understand the appropriate responses in each case.

Step Five: Sequencing Instruction

Although the librarians would have little control over how an individual instructor incorporated the library unit into the overall sequence of the class, the workbook itself would follow the familiar learning cycle pattern for learners with no background (illustrated in Figure 6.20). Instruction would begin with the explaining phase, in which an overview of the search strategy students will be following is presented. Next, a particular step in the procedure would be described, followed by an application, in which an example of a source that could be used in that step is given. Then the student would select a source for his or her own topic in an experience phase. The examining phase would depend a great deal on the extent to which the course instructor took class time to discuss students' problems, questions, and experiences. The workbook could contain a section after each phase in which students recorded problems they had in accomplishing that step. Whoever would be responsible for reviewing the workbook could then provide feedback on those portions of the workbook.

If the attitude clarification method is used for the affective objectives, it follows the learning cycle from experiencing (based on students' responses to the questionnaire items), to examining (when students work in groups to discuss the group's responses to an item), to explaining (when the instructor gives out the "answers," indicating which would be considered the best reasoned response), to applying (when the students go back over their own responses and determine where their attitudes have changed).

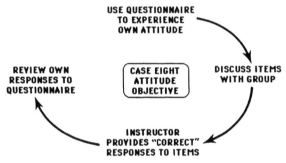

Figure 6.20   Instructional sequence for Case Eight.

Step Six: Checking for Continuity with Learning Principles

The motivational factors for this design hinge on two factors. First, the library unit should be assigned in conjunction with a real paper assignment, thus creating a need to know on the part of the students. Second, the workbook materials should focus on the students' chosen topic, rather than requiring them to learn all the sources. This specialization should tap into any pre-existing motivation about the topic. A third source of motivation, which may or may not be functional, is the provision for frequent feedback in the workbook. The students are actively involved in finding information and can see that they are making progress toward their goal. This is often very motivating for beginning students.

The organization for this material is primarily reflected in the design of the workbook. It should be a clearly outlined step-by-step approach which will lead the students through the procedures. They should have no difficulty discriminating between the purposes of the various parts, and the parts should be easily discriminated from one another as well. Something that might facilitate the discriminability is the color coding of the various parts as was suggested in Case Six.

The methods suggested for this case are built on the notion of active responding and require that the students make notations in the workbooks as they go along. These notations then become the basis for their papers in class and are, therefore, very relevant to their class work. This is different from many workbook approaches in which the responses stand alone in a vacuum with no connection to anything else the students are doing.

The only problem with this approach comes in the feedback phase. Because the responses are tailored to the students' own needs, it is impossible to build into the workbook feedback on the accuracy of the responses. The feedback must come from the apparent progress which is being made and from later review of the materials by the instructor. While this is not the most desirable situation, it can be acceptable, provided the instructor does not delay the feedback too long into the process. The librarians can suggest that in the initial stages of the use of the workbook the instructor make weekly checks on student progress. The frequency of the checks can then be reduced as the semester progresses.

This case is based on a real-life situation; see Schwartz and Burton (1981) for additional information on this approach.

IN SUMMARY

The cases just described attempt to cover a range of situations a librarian might face and a range of solutions to consider. We have deliberately avoided "standard" solutions in an attempt to be creative and inspire you to be the same. Granted, these descriptions wouldn't work for everyone, but we hope they indicate some possibilities that might not have occurred to you as well as illustrate how the design process can help stimulate the instructor's thinking.

As you can see from the discussion of these cases, this process is not an exact step-by-step procedure; there is no one best way of designing instruction just as there is no one best way of finding information. Taking into consideration all of the variables, regardless of the order, will result in a better instructional design. The more you do it, the easier the process becomes.

Now let's look at how these and other instructional sequences might be evaluated.

REFERENCE

Schwartz, B. A., and Burton, S. (1981). *Teaching Library Skills in Freshman English: An Undergraduate Library's Experience.* Contributions to Librarianship, No. 6, University of Texas at Austin, The General Libraries, Austin, Texas.

7
Assessing the Effectiveness of Instruction

For many of us involved in teaching, the most formidable aspect of the instructional design process is evaluation. We tend to think of it only in terms of elaborately constructed research projects involving pre- and post-tests, control and experimental groups, and results reported in chi-square, t-tests, and other statistical measures with equally unappealing names. Evaluation can be this complex, but it doesn't have to be. A range of possibilities is available to us, and not all of them require inordinate amounts of time and extensive training in statistics.

Evaluation can be undertaken for many reasons: to compare different instructional methods, to assess the effectiveness of the instructor, to improve the instructional unit, to determine the effect of instruction on students' library behavior, to assess students' opinion about the library or the instructional sequence, or to find out if students learned what we set out to teach them. This last reason, the assessment of learning, is the focus of this chapter.

As we proceed, we will analyze the evaluation methods typically applied to library instruction, the factors to consider in choosing a method, and the use of evaluation results in revising instruction. Although we will not discuss how to construct particular types of evaluation instruments, we will include an example of each type. For guidance on the construction of evaluation instruments, see Sax (1980).

FORMAL EVALUATION METHODS

To lay the foundation for the rest of this chapter, definitions of the terminology applied to evaluation instruments are in order. Educators, psychologists, and others who work with testing and evaluation stress the importance of three qualities in any measurement device: *validity, reliability*, and *usability*.

Validity, the most important of these characteristics, refers to the extent to which a test or other instrument measures what it is supposed to measure. This concept is sometimes called the *truthfulness* of an instrument. However, a test can only be valid for the purpose for which it was intended. For example, an English grammar test that is valid for measuring students' knowledge of grammar rules would not be a valid test of students' writing ability. Likewise, a test that focuses on definitions of library terminology would not be a valid measure of students' ability to apply information-gathering skills in a library. The key to validity, then, is the connection between test items and the instructional objectives of the unit. Unless the measurement device is closely tied to the content of the unit, the instrument cannot yield a valid measure of students' attainment of the unit's instructional objectives.

Reliability refers to the degree to which an evaluation instrument yields consistent results. An instrument is reliable if we obtain similar results for each student under either of these conditions: 1) when the same instrument is administered repeatedly to the same students, or 2) when different raters score the same students with the same instrument. A measuring device can be reliable in terms of giving consistent scores but not valid for the purpose in which it is being used; however, it cannot be valid if it is not reliable because we cannot depend on the score obtained to stay the same.

The third characteristic, *usability*, refers to the practicality of an instrument, that is, the ease with which it can be constructed, administered, and scored. A test that is high in both validity and reliability can be worthless if the time needed to construct it is disproportionate to the usefulness of the test's results.

In summary, then, "a good measuring instrument measures what it is supposed to measure to a high degree, consistently, and with a minimum expenditure of time, energy, and money" (Ross and Stanley, 1954). As we describe each evaluation method that can be used to assess learning, we will consider how it measures up to this maxim.

Objective Tests

Definition and Use

Perhaps the most familiar method of evaluating achievement of library skills is the objective test. It is sometimes called a *selected response* test because the student *chooses* from among several alternative answers. The term *objective* refers to the scoring of the answers, which can be done almost automatically (each question has only one correct answer), rather than to any objectivity or fairness of the items themselves. Objective tests are typically given immediately following instruction, although they can be incorporated into the instruction itself to measure progress as learning occurs. In the latter case, the test is built into each module, as in computer-assisted instruction, programmed instruction, or an audiotutorial. For example, the CAI unit for the on-line catalog training described in Case Two in the previous chapter and the tour exercise for freshman English students in Case Eight both would incorporate this type of evaluation.

Appendix A gives some examples of objective test items for library objectives involving student preparation for an on-line search that could be executed by library staff. Note that we would not recommend giving this test to the graduate nutrition students doing an on-line search in Case Seven, even though the objectives are very similar; an objective test does not fit the teaching methods selected for the case, the students, or the main objective of the instruction. Other evaluation methods which are discussed later in this chapter would be more appropriate for Case Seven.

Validity
There is no guarantee that, by its very nature, an objective test is going to be more valid than other types of tests. In fact, its validity as a measure of skill objectives is not as good as other types of tests. The best use of an objective test is for cognitive skills at the basic levels. It can be designed to test more advanced cognitive objectives, but this use takes some practice on the instructor's part. Regardless of the level of objectives, the best way to insure the validity of objective tests is to keep the questions very closely tied to the instructional objectives.

Reliability

One of the strong points of objective tests is their reliability. Because there are few judgments necessary in the scoring (did the student mark the correct space or not?), scoring can be made automatic. When scoring of a question can be so carefully specified that you can get a machine to do it, you have eliminated one source of interference with reliability.

Machine scoring does not guarantee that an objective test *will* be reliable, since there are other factors affecting its reliability. They include ambiguity in the way the questions are worded, degree of clarity of the alternative choices for each item, and so on, as well as student variables over which the instructor has no control. On the whole, however, it is fair to say that an objective test has a higher possibility for reliability than all other forms of evaluation.

Usability

Objective tests have a high degree of usability for a variety of reasons. First, they take much less time to administer than most other forms of evaluation. The actual response time on the part of the students is minimal; all their time is spent in thinking about and choosing among the alternatives. Second, it is easy to vary the time needed by varying the number of items asked. You can give a three-question test or a fifty-question test, depending on the amount of time you have available. Third, the scoring time is minimal for the instructor. In fact, it is easy enough to have the students score their own tests and to use the occasion as a learning experience for them. Whether or not you would actually do this would depend a great deal on why the test was being administered. Much as we hate to say this, if the test counts for a grade, the students probably shouldn't score their own papers. If, however, the test is for feedback only, it's even more effective to have the students score their own. Fourth, the results of these tests can be quantified and used for comparisons of students' knowledge before and after instruction.

Objective tests have several drawbacks, however. They are difficult and time-consuming to construct if they are done well. This is especially true for advanced cognitive questions. Unambiguous questions (those that have only one possible answer) are sometimes hard to write. For the results to be meaningful, the questions have to be tested statistically for both validity and reliability, which is sometimes difficult to do for a one-shot testing situation.

To avoid the pitfalls of local construction, many librarians look to published (standardized) tests, which have already undergone the statistical screening process. These, however, are not without their problems, chief of which is the fact that a published test will be a valid measure for your situation only if the questions reflect the content of your instruction and the test was designed for the same use you intend to make of it. In addition, published tests tend to measure students' recall of facts (e.g., definitions of library terminology, identification of elements of card catalog and index entries, call number arrangement, and the like), rather than students' ability to apply information-gathering procedures or use analysis, synthesis, and evaluation skills. Finally, a wide range of published library skills tests for college-level students is not readily available.

Essay Tests

Definition and Use
Essay tests contain open-ended questions that students answer in their own words. These are also called *constructed response* tests because the student must construct an answer rather than select one from a list of alternatives. This type of test also includes short-

answer questions. The longer the required response, the less likely the possibility that only one correct answer exists for each question because the questions are generally more complex. Although inefficient for measuring knowledge of facts, essay tests can be used more effectively to assess learning of more advanced cognitive objectives: application, analysis, synthesis, and evaluation. This format is especially useful in cases where evidence of the process the student used in obtaining an answer is as important as the answer itself. Questions that require students to solve problems or to make judgments or comparisons are an effective use of this kind of instrument. For example, an essay test could be used in Case Three in the previous chapter with advanced science students who might be asked to critique the search strategy decision-making described in students' journals from previous semesters.

An example of essay questions for a library skills unit also appears in Appendix A. The instructional objectives are the same as those used for the objective test items, to allow for comparison.

Validity
Because the types of behavior that can be evaluated in essay tests closely mirror the requirements of real-life problem-solving, the validity of essay tests tends to be greater than that of objective tests. Essay questions require the learner to recall and sort a great deal of information with very few external cues, a situation much like that faced with a real information question. Objective questions, in comparison, require the learner to choose from among a set of alternative answers, a situation not often provided in the real world.

However, writing questions that closely parallel the unit's instructional objectives is not as easy as it might seem, and this parallelism is the only readily accessible way of judging the valid-

ity of an essay test because all other procedures are very complicated.

Reliability

Unfortunately, although essay tests may have more validity, they
fall down seriously when it comes to reliability. Several factors
contribute to this problem. First, scoring essay tests is very difficult. It is time-consuming and subject to a great many sources of
bias and error, which automatically lower the reliability of the
test. Use of a rating scale or answer key that highlights the desired elements in each answer can produce a more standard analysis. However, whether or not a standard is used, results can be influenced by many factors such as students' writing ability, position of the student's paper in the grading sequence, grader fatigue,
and more. Second, the time involved in answering essay items
means that fewer items can be included on a single test, which also
means that less of the student's behavior is being sampled. The result is lower reliability.

Usability

Some of the factors influencing the usability of essay tests have already been mentioned. It is an easy form of evaluation to administer, but the scoring is time-consuming and difficult. That makes
it impossible for students to score their own tests in class as they
can with objective tests; feedback, therefore, must be delayed. On
the other hand, because short questions usually have a more
focused answer, they can be administered and self-evaluated on a
very general basis and used as feedback in class. Any serious or extensive evaluation of answers must wait until the instructor can sit
and grade the tests.

Worksheets

Definition and Use

A worksheet is an outline of the steps of a process students are
supposed to complete, along with space for them to document

their findings. It can focus on an entire search strategy or the use of a particular reference source. For example, students might be asked to select an index appropriate to their topic, write down the title of the index, note the subject headings used for the topic, list the relevant articles that are indexed in one volume, and, after reading several articles, evaluate the usefulness of the index for the topic.

Worksheets are completed during the instructional sequence rather than at the end of it. They are often part of workbooks and can be used with other indirect methods of instruction such as study guides and simulations and with more advanced objectives such as application. Some instructors use a form of worksheet in a lecture situation, which is often called a set of *controlled notes*. These notes ask the student to respond to questions throughout the course of the lecture by writing down notes on the worksheet.

We saw in Case Five and Seven in the previous chapter how worksheets were used with engineering students gathering information for writing a specification and nutrition students preparing for an on-line search. The worksheet that appears in Appendix B was developed for use by freshman English students at the University of Texas at Austin, a scenario that closely resembles that described in Case Eight. This worksheet outlines the steps students are to follow in finding information for their library papers: from background information in encyclopedias, to books found through the library's subject catalog, to periodical articles located through periodical indexes and the library's serial records. The objectives for the library unit, which is administered by the Undergraduate Library, are the same as those in Case Eight.

Validity
Like essay tests, worksheets are based on the actual responses a learner will need to make in accomplishing a given objective. There-

fore, they will tend to be fairly valid, depending on the care given to their construction. Responses required should be significant components of the activity being learned and not just convenient markers. Use of the latter will detract from the validity of the method.

Because students complete the process as they fill in the worksheet, they can more easily demonstrate their mastery of the instructional objectives, as long as the content of the worksheet is relevant to the content of the instruction. This relevance enhances the validity of this form of evaluation. Compared to an essay test that might ask students to *describe* a search strategy they would follow under certain circumstances, for example, a worksheet that requires students to actually *use* library resources to complete it is a more direct measure of students' performance in the library. However, the actual behavior itself is not observed; we must rely on the precision in student reporting as proof of their mastery. This does not affect the validity, but can affect reliability.

Reliability
Like formal tests, worksheets are difficult to construct because they require clearly written, precise instructions for both the steps students are expected to follow in completing the process and the information they are expected to record. Ambiguous directions will increase the amount of variability in the students' answers and detract from the reliability of the evaluation.

Another source of problems in reliability arises when we use a worksheet that documents students' information-finding skills on topics of their own choosing rather than on a preset topic. The former tends to be a more subjective evaluation instrument because the possible responses are so much broader. In this case, the instructor rarely has an answer key, so scoring tends to be even more inconsistent, time-consuming, and difficult to handle with large groups. Each response must be treated individually and cannot be readily compared with other students' responses. Results are not easily quantified.

Assessing student performance on this type of evaluation suffers from many of the same grading problems that plague essay tests. One advantage that worksheets have over essays is that the answers tend to be shorter and less ambiguous, making grading somewhat easier. However, a great deal will depend on the amount of care taken to make the questions and instructions clear.

Usability

While worksheets may have several drawbacks as formal evaluation instruments, they do provide a way of keeping the student actively involved in the learning, a virtue alluded to in our chapter on learning theory. It is difficult to strike a balance between tailoring the learning to the needs of the individual student and making the instructions clear and unambiguous enough to be followed easily. Instructions that are too cut and dried might bore students and appear to be busy work rather than a valuable learning experience. However, if the worksheet is made challenging enough by allowing students to vary the process according to their own needs and interests, then it becomes an even more difficult grading task.

Journals

Definition and Use

Like the worksheet, the journal is used to document the process students followed in their research while the research was in progress. The journal differs from the worksheet in its lack of explicit structure. Typically, students are asked to record what sources they used, in what order, and why; how useful these sources were for their projects; what problems they encountered and how they resolved them; and so forth. The science students in Case Three in the previous chapter were asked to keep a journal of their research so the librarian and course instructor could identify problem areas; their journals could also be used to evaluate the completeness and efficiency of the process the students followed to find information for their papers.

A sample set of journal guidelines and entries for an introductory sociology course is found in Appendix C.

Validity
Journals can provide a fairly realistic picture of the information-gathering techniques used by students and the reasoning behind their behavior; thus journals would tend to be fairly valid measures of these skills. However, the instructor must give the students extensive guidelines for the entries in order for the journals to provide information on the skills the instructor intends them to measure. The guidelines for student entries must closely parallel the unit's instructional objectives.

Reliability
Journals are subject to all the same sources of unreliability as essay tests and worksheets. First, we must depend on the students' ability to report their own behavior accurately. Even with criteria for student entries and for those evaluating journals, rating is extremely subjective and time-consuming, producing fairly unreliable results. Here again, as with the essay test, the results can be influenced by students' writing ability and other non-content variables.

Usability
The journal is an attractive activity from a learning standpoint because it encourages active learning and reflection on that learning by the students. Most journals are designed to force the students to think about why they are making certain choices. This approach should cause them to have a better understanding of what they are learning, especially in light of the learning cycle described

in Chapter 4. However, in this section, we are discussing the use of journals as an evaluation device, and with that in mind, our assessment is not as enthusiastic.

The biggest problem with journals is compliance. The librarian and the course instructor must cooperate to motivate the students to take the assignment seriously. Most librarians do not have sufficient exposure to a single class to allow them to enforce completion of the journal. Journal use requires interaction over a longer period of time than a single class session, which can be a serious drawback for many librarians.

As with all forms of constructed-response evaluation, journals require a great deal of time from both the students and the instructor. This requirement must be considered if you are thinking about using journals as an evaluation technique. Will the students have the time and inclination to complete the process? Will you have the time to evaluate their products? And is the probable payoff of evaluating their learning worth the time that must be invested?

Performance Tests (Process Analysis)

Definition and Use
If the instructional sequence calls for students to be able to do something rather than just answer questions about doing it, a performance test can be used. Here the instructor relies on actual, rather than reported, behavior; he or she watches each student closely and rates the student's performance of the task. Performance tests are particularly effective for assessing students' ability to perform a procedure, either cognitive or psychomotor.

There are several situations in which a performance test should be considered: 1) where the steps in the process are more important than the final results; 2) where there is no tangible

product; or 3) where the outcome of the process can't be pre-
dicted because it varies with the steps in the process. For example,
assessing students' ability to use OCLC fits all three criteria: inability to document the steps in a process, lack of a tangible product,
and unpredictable outcomes. Appendix D contains a sample
checklist for a performance test that assesses students' use of
OCLC to determine if the library has a particular book.

Another example of the use of a performance test might be
found in Case Two in the previous chapter. Here, as part of the
CAI unit, if the learner was given the opportunity to actually use
the on-line catalog, as suggested in the case, this module could incorporate a performance test, although the monitoring would be
done by the computer instead of a live instructor. The computer
program could include a checklist of the proper sequence of steps
needed to complete the task assigned and then compare the learner's steps with that checklist.

Validity
Most performance tests are highly valid measures of the instructional objectives because they ask for direct performance of the
desired result. One way to detract from their validity is to test the
behavior under conditions that are not the same as those in either
the instruction or the actual practice setting. For example, if we
teach you to do an OCLC search using a particular type of computer but test you on a different computer, the change in the test
setting reduces the validity of that test of your learning because
we're not really testing you on what we had you learn.

Another way to lower the validity of a performance test is
to decide to observe aspects of performance that are not really
matched to the instructional objectives. For example, if we are
trying to teach you to use good form in serving a tennis ball, but
the measure we use is where you place the ball on the court, that

would not be a valid measure of your form because it is possible to have good ball placement even with bad form. In other words, selection of the tasks to be performed greatly affects the test's validity. The behavior chosen must also be an adequate sample of the instructional objectives.

Reliability

Performance tests are subject to many of the same reliability problems as essays, worksheets, and journals. For students' behavior to be judged appropriately, the instructor should have a rating scale or checklist that highlights the steps in the procedure, to increase the reliability of scoring.

Usability

Perhaps the biggest drawback to performance tests as evaluation instruments is the fact that they are administered on a one-to-one basis. Therefore, only a short procedure or a part of a longer one can be evaluated in a class of any size.

Another drawback to performance tests is that administering them can be difficult. The instructor needs to control the situation, so that each student is examined under the same conditions, and present the task clearly, so that everyone understands the directions.

One advantage of performance tests is that the rating takes place while the test is being administered and, therefore, there is no out-of-class time needed for either the students or the instructor. On the other hand, performance tests will consume a great deal of class time. They are probably more feasible in the individual tutoring situation rather than in the classroom.

Bibliographies/Research Papers (Product Analysis)

Definition and Use

As a product of students' research, the paper can be a useful evaluation device if the end result is more important than the process that led to it. However, evaluation of the product alone will yield little, if any, clues about the process. If you use product analysis, you have to accept the product as evidence of the correct completion of the process; if you cannot make that assumption, you have to evaluate the process instead, either by asking students to document it or by using a performance test. The message here is this: If search strategy is your emphasis, evaluation of only the product is not necessarily a valid measure of students' ability to complete the process you have taught, unless you do extensive studies to show that one can't produce a good paper without a good search.

In product analysis, some evaluators consider only the bibliography, while others judge the quality of the research paper as a whole. The bibliography can be evaluated according to criteria such as the number of sources used, their level (scholarly vs. popular), the diversity of sources (books vs. periodicals, primary vs. secondary), the timeliness of sources, the format of citations, and so forth. These same criteria can be applied to the entire research paper, with the additional consideration given to how well the facts and opinions were incorporated into it.

Finding information and then using it are the two components of writing a research paper. As librarians, we tend to focus exclusively on the information-gathering aspect; many course instructors, especially those in English departments, would be more interested in how the information is used. A sample rating scale for a freshman English research paper is found in Appendix E; both components are included in it.

Five of the cases in the previous chapter incorporated product analysis: the urban planning class (Case One), the science honors class (Case Three), the civil engineering class (Case Five), the nutrition class (Case Seven), and the freshman English class

(Case Eight). In all but Case One, the students documented the process they used to gather information. Although the engineering students didn't write a research paper or proposal like the others mentioned here, their specification-writing assignment did lead to a product that incorporated the students' findings in the library.

Validity

We have already mentioned that the use of the research paper as a measure of search strategy requires a leap of faith. We are making the assumption that the paper presented is an accurate reflection of the library skills it is intended to measure and couldn't have been produced without them. We are also assuming that it was this particular student whose work is reflected in this paper—another issue altogether.

Reliability

In product evaluation, as in process evaluation, use of a checklist or rating scale increases the reliability of scoring. The fact that the students are usually writing papers on a variety of topics adds to the difficulty of producing reliable scoring, since there are many more variables that could have affected the students' performance.

Usability

Because production of the paper is outside of the instructional setting, the time and situational constraints that made performance tests so difficult to administer are not present here. Aside from preparing a rating scale or checklist and informing students of the criteria for grading when the paper is assigned, no other advance preparation is necessary. In fact, in many settings, the librarian is not involved in grading at all: that part of the process belongs to the course instructor. If, however, the papers are being used to provide feedback to the librarian on the effectiveness of instruction, then he or she will want to evaluate the students' products for that reason. Then the time-consumption factor and

the difficulty in making inferences about library behavior from
an end product become important considerations.

INFORMAL METHODS FOR ASSESSING
STUDENT LEARNING

The methods discussed above are fairly formal procedures for finding out if the students have learned anything. They would be useful in those situations in which you need documentation about
learning. But many times, such documentation is not necessary;
you are gathering evidence of student progress for your own benefit or that of the course instructor only. In these instances, less
formal evaluation methods are more practical and less intrusive.
Here are some you might consider.

Observation

Observation is sometimes called *measurement without instruments*
(Bradfield and Moredock, 1957). It is an unstructured method of
evaluation in comparison to performance tests, which rely on
structured behavior. It occurs during instruction or in the library
itself as students attempt to apply skills taught in class.

Here are some observations which can be made and might
be useful:

1)   What kinds of questions do students ask in class?
2)   What kinds of questions can students answer in class?
3)   What kinds of questions do students ask in the library proper?
4)   What problems do students have with the concepts covered in
     the instruction once they start to apply them?

There are obviously many more questions that an instructor
can watch for during learning: Those listed above are just examples.

The primary focus in observation is that the instructor watches the students' behavior rather than obtaining a test score or product that is supposed to be indicative of that behavior; students' actions are appraised as they occur.

Because it usually relies solely on the perceptions of the evaluator without any record of an individual's performance and because it cannot be done very systematically, observation is less reliable than more formal evaluation techniques. As with performance tests, the use of rating scales, checklists, or even anecdotal records can enhance reliability. However, observation should be used only when a more reliable method is not available.

Apart from its reliability shortcomings, observation can be misleading. For example, even if librarians can accurately identify students in the library who have had the instructional sequence under evaluation, one student with a question is not an accurate sample; he or she may be the only one who had that question. In the classroom, students' nonverbal behavior can be misinterpreted as a lack of comprehension when it is in fact boredom or lack of interest. Observed behavior can often indicate something other than achievement; unless the observed behavior can be tied specifically to the instructional objectives, what is observed is not a valid measure of students' attainment of those objectives. Observation is less useful in assessing learning than in determining the quality of instruction or ways to improve it.

Self-Report

Sometimes in our quest for the perfect evaluation system, we forget that we are dealing with thinking, self-analytical human beings. In the absence of more rigorous alternatives, it might be just as satisfactory to ask the students how they think they're doing. This is not the type of evaluation you would use to assess learning in any formal sense, but it could be used during the course of instruction to get a feel for how things are progressing. Of course, anyone choosing this method should take all results with a grain of salt and eventually back up any observations with a more rigorous measure. But as a temporary testing of the waters, student self-reports can be useful.

Conversations with Faculty

Course instructors are a good source of information on either students' reactions to instruction after it has taken place or the impact of the instructional sequence on students' class performance (e.g., the quality of their papers or speeches). However, unless the course instructors are directly involved in evaluating the process or product of instruction, they cannot accurately assess students' learning. Even when they do grade students' papers, as we discussed earlier, course instructors tend to do so from a different perspective, which might not match the objectives of the librarian.

CHOOSING A METHOD

With all of these possibilities available to you, then, how do you go about choosing a method for evaluation? Several factors that affect your decision must be considered: your reasons for doing the evaluation, the type and level of your instructional objectives, the students' characteristics, and your situational constraints. If all but the first one sound familiar, it's because these are the same factors you considered in selecting a teaching method. You can apply the information you gathered then to this step of the instructional design process. We will look at each of these factors in turn as they relate to choosing an evaluation method, and we will introduce a new concept: your reasons for doing the evaluation.

Why Are You Doing the Evaluation?

Before you can make any decisions regarding a method, you have
to decide why you are doing the evaluation. Who will receive your
results, and what will those individuals want to know? How will
each party gauge the success of your instructional unit? To answer
these questions, let's look at four possible audiences and the
points each is likely to consider. These audiences are the students,
the course instructor, the librarian, and the administration.

The Students

Perhaps the most immediate need for assessing learning is to provide students with feedback concerning their achievement of the
stated objectives. In Chapter 5, we discussed the importance of
feedback in the learning process: Positive feedback strengthens
the student's response, and negative feedback corrects it. Each
student will want to know the following: How well did I do? How
did my score compare with the class average? In which areas do I
need the most improvement?

The Course Instructor

The course instructor may be interested in group, rather than
individual, achievement, unless the evaluation results will affect
each student's grade in the course. For example, what percentage
of students achieved the objectives? What level of skills did the
students attain? Faculty may also be looking for evidence that
demonstrates the value of library instruction to their courses and
students. You may need to answer the following questions to sus-
tain or increase faculty support of your efforts: How will attainment of these library skills contribute to the course's goals? Was
the time spent on library instruction a good use of limited class
time?

The Librarian

The librarian is also going to be interested in how well the students did, but from a different point of view. In an instructional

capacity, the librarian will be looking for indications that the instructional sequence needs revision. Specific questions might include the following: What areas gave students trouble? How did students feel about the experience? What was the faculty's reaction? How can I improve instruction?

The Administration

Because administrators at both the library and institutional levels are removed from the immediate instructional situation, they are less likely to be concerned with student achievement than with the following considerations: How much does this program cost? Is it worth the time, money, staff, and other resources committed to the program? What has been the response of faculty and students? How does the instructional unit contribute to the library's and institution's goals?

In Summary

Although we have focused on using evaluation to determine if students are learning what the unit is trying to teach, the results can be used in a variety of settings in accordance with the needs of each audience: to provide students with feedback, to improve instruction, to gain faculty support, and to justify the program to the library and institution's administrations.

These different audiences require different types and quality of data. Once you have established your audience, you will have to then consider what kind of data will be required to achieve your aim for that audience. It would be fairly safe to say that, no matter who the audience is, a component of the information which will be needed is some measure of student learning, such as those we have been discussing. The questions then become how precise must the data be, how much detail on individuals is needed, how quickly must the data be available, and many others. For example, if you want to secure increased funding for your program, will the administrators require hard data on student learning or will they be swayed by descriptions of student achievement in more general terms, accompanied by supporting faculty and student comments? If the data are being collected for your own benefit to improve instruction, you would be more interested in attitudes and problems encountered than in how much each student actually learned. Thus the choice of methods for gathering information on student learning would depend on the eventual use of that information.

The Objectives

Just as instructional objectives form the foundation of decision-making for selecting a teaching method, so do they influence the selection of an evaluation method. Each type of instrument is suitable for particular types of objectives: Mismatching the two could invalidate evaluation results. Figure 7.1 presents a chart that pairs evaluation methods with instructional objective types.

The most efficient means of assessing basic cognitive objectives is through objective testing. Intermediate objectives present a greater choice: Objective tests, essay tests, worksheets, and performance tests would be appropriate. If the instructional sequence focuses on advanced cognitive objectives, you can choose from objective tests, essay tests, worksheets, journals, and product analysis. Essay tests are particularly useful for objectives that require the student to form an opinion or combine things in a novel way; product analysis works well for situations in which principles are applied to new settings. A performance test is relevant for assessing psychomotor skills. It is possible to use some forms of objective test items, such as multiple choice, for almost all levels, but the item-construction process in those cases increases in difficulty as the level increases in complexity.

	BASIC COGNITIVE	INTERMEDIATE COGNITIVE	COMPLEX COGNITIVE	PSYCHO-MOTOR
OBJECTIVE TESTS	+	+	+	
ESSAY TESTS		+	+	
WORKSHEETS		+	+	
JOURNALS			+	
PRODUCT ANALYSIS			+	
PROCESS ANALYSIS		+		+

Figure 7.1 Appropriateness of various evaluation methods for different objectives.

We have omitted affective objectives from the chart in Figure 7.1 and from the previous discussion in this chapter because few library-skills instructional sequences deal with affective objectives exclusively. For this reason, assessment of these objectives can be incorporated into whatever evaluation device is chosen for the unit. Essay tests, for example, which work well with several types of cognitive objectives, can also be employed in assessing the affective domain. If you are using objective tests, you can include some scaled items in which students are asked to select the statement that best describes their attitudes about some topic. In worksheets, journals, and other written measures, questions about student reactions can be added to the instruction sheet. Only in the case of performance tests or end-product evaluation does it become difficult to match the affective evaluation format to the cognitive format. In each of those cases, affective objectives are usually observed in the care with which a task is completed and the enthusiasm with which it is approached.

As unlikely as it may seem, in some situations, the objectives may dictate that no evaluation is needed. An example of such an instance would be in the freshman history class described in Case Four in the previous chapter, where basic cognitive and affective objectives were the focus of instruction. As you may recall, the librarian in this case used a series of activities to highlight the services offered by the college library and how it differed from other libraries the students were familiar with, all the while portraying the library as a wonderful facility for students. The enthusiasm and goodwill toward libraries and librarians that was generated by these activities would be dissipated quickly if the students were faced with any type of test.

The Situation

After instructional objectives, the most significant influence on your choice of evaluation methods is situational constraints. These factors include time, class size, and facilities.

When class time is at a premium, you may need to choose one of the methods that can be administered outside of class: journals, worksheets, or product analysis. An alternative is to incorporate short evaluations into the instruction itself, which has the added advantage of making learning more active and providing more immediate feedback. Performance tests are particularly unwieldy with a large group or an extensive procedure because each student must be observed individually. At the same time, grading the journals, worksheets, products, or essay tests of a large group may also be difficult because they all require subjective analysis.

Finally, if special facilities are required for administering the evaluation, as in a performance test, your lack of equipment would limit your choices.

The Students

We have seen in Figure 7.1 that several options exist for intermediate and complex cognitive objectives. You can narrow your choices by considering the characteristics of your students. Variables would include factors such as students' motivation level, their sophistication level, and their background, just as in choosing a teaching method.

For example, journals might not be an appropriate method for assessing achievement of students with low-level motivation because these students might require a more structured situation; lack of motivation would affect the results. On the other hand, journals can be extremely useful in situations where students have varying levels of experience in using the library because journals allow students to record not only their behavior but also their reasoning behind it. Journals also allow the instructor to tailor the evaluation more to the student's ability level.

In Summary

Choosing an evaluation method is a lot like choosing a teaching method: No single method fits all situations and no single situation fits all methods. And more than one method can be used in many instances. In fact, multiple measures are desirable, especially in classroom settings where a process under immediate study and a final product that is produced later are both evaluated. Much of what is taught in library instruction produces a tangible product; it is not uncommon for the librarian to evaluate students' progress with a workbook or simulation that teaches a search strategy and then grade their research papers as well. Multiple measures provide greater reliability because they offer assessment from different perspectives, and it is a fact of measurement that the more information you have, the more reliable and valid the evaluation will be.

USING EVALUATION RESULTS TO REVISE INSTRUCTION

While the evaluation methods we have discussed in this chapter can be used to determine whether students have learned what we have tried to teach them, the results of our evaluation efforts can be employed to improve instruction. Students' performance on a formal evaluation is an indication of the soundness of the design of an instructional sequence. Coupled with students' reactions to the instruction while it is taking place, results of their performance can be analyzed to assess the appropriateness of instructional objectives, teaching methods, and evaluation methods.

If evaluation results signal a problem in instructional design, several factors could be at the root of the problem. Perhaps the instructional objectives were inappropriate for the group of learners. The students might have been more sophisticated than was expected. Or, alternatively, the students didn't have the prerequisite skills or knowledge the librarian assumed in planning the unit. This problem is common in two types of settings: 1) those that don't have a program of library skills instruction, where objectives can be formulated for different stages in the program; and 2) those that have a high number of transfer students, where students in any one class haven't attained the same level of experience in using the library. If you are not sure at what level to set your objectives, consider administering a needs assessment to determine the group's level of expertise prior to instruction. Then if there are students without the necessary prerequisites, individual instructional methods could be used to bring them up to the level of the rest of the class. Or, if students are more sophisticated than expected, you are in the delightful position of being able to teach more or at a higher level than you expected.

Another common problem with objectives is not in the level but the number for the time allotted. When an instructor attempts to teach too many concepts in the amount of time available, students may not be able to attain all of them. It is wise not to try to include more than one major concept for every ten to fifteen minutes of time. It should be remembered, however, that well-organized material will allow more to be included because it is the organization which will aid in memory.

Another possible problem in instructional design can be in the choice of teaching method. Perhaps it was inappropriate for the type and level of instructional objectives or perhaps it wasn't a method that was compatible with the instructor's strengths. Sometimes the method doesn't lend itself to the situation in which the instruction is taking place. All of these factors will impact how well students will learn.

Aside from the instructional design, the evaluation method itself might be at fault. If it isn't valid for the intended purpose, the results will be meaningless. If the method is valid but not the best measure for the stated objectives, the information gained will not help in decision-making. If the best method for the content is impeded by situational constraints, the instructor may just have to settle for a less appropriate method and accept the fact that you can't always get what you want.

Even the most carefully planned instructional sequence is likely to need some revision after it is administered the first time.

In fact, every instructor should plan on changing some aspect of a new library skills unit at least once. In reality, revision is often ongoing, as students, curricula, faculty, and library policies and programs change.

REFERENCES

Bradfield, J. M., and Moredock, H. S. (1957). *Measurement and Evaluation in Education*, Macmillan, New York, p. 48.

Ross, C. C., and Stanley, J. C. (1954). *Measurement in Today's Schools*, Prentice-Hall, Englewood Cliffs, New Jersey, p. 131.

Sax, G. (1980). *Principles of Educational and Psychological Measurement and Evaluation*, 2nd ed., Wadsworth Publishing Co., Belmont, California.

8
Some Golden Rules of Design

Now we have reached the end of the instructional design process. At this point, it seems fairly formidable: There's so much to consider. It *is* formidable; anything worthwhile always seems that way when taken in big chunks like this. It's like learning to drive. When you first start, you have to remember to buckle the seat belt, turn the key while lightly touching the gas, put the car in drive, and on and on. And it's even worse with a standard transmission. You thought you'd never get it all memorized, much less coordinated. Now look at you. You can do the whole sequence without a hitch and carry on a conversation, plan your day, tune the radio, or any number of other activities at the same time.

Take heart. Going through the instructional design process will eventually become as easy and automatic for you as driving a car or locating a book on the shelves. It just takes practice and repetition and a willingness to try. In fact, after a while, it becomes almost difficult to dissect the process into its separate steps because they begin to influence one another so rapidly. At first, however, you'll need to step carefully through the process as we outlined it in the overview, beginning with the objectives and ending with a revision process which keeps the instruction fresh.

It should be obvious by this point that we have certain special favorites among the pages of advice on instructional design. Therefore, we'd like to conclude by highlighting a few which would serve as a good starting point. We refer to them as our "Golden Rules of Instructional Design." We hope they make the process a little easier for you.

The most blatant of our biases is that the specification of the objectives is the pivotal step in the design process. The decision on the objectives influences all subsequent decisions. Too often we find instructors who look at the instructional situation and throw their hands up in despair:

"I only have fifty minutes; I can't do anything besides lecture."

"I have so much to cover and so little time."

We can list a great many of these cries of despair. How much more the students would learn if the instructor thought about the objectives first and tried to find a clever way of achieving them rather than assuming it can't be done. So our first golden rule of instructional design is this:

Let the objective drive the design, not the other way around.

and its corollary:

Be creative!

Don't use a particular instructional method just because it's always been done that way. First of all, it may be wrong for your objectives or your students or this setting or you. Second, while doing the same thing all the time may save time, it can also lead to boredom on the part of the instructor. As we learned in Chapter 5, an unenthusiastic instructor can kill the enthusiasm of the students, if any exists. So you owe it to yourself and to your students to keep yourself and your material fresh. Even Henny Youngman uses new material every now and then.

And now a more radical theme we've been emphasizing, if subtly, throughout our discussions:

Make the students do some of the work.

Of course, prior to this, we've put this point in more positive phrasing like "active responding is good for learning." But from a strictly selfish viewpoint, making the students do some of the work in class is a good idea. After all, you can't learn the material for them; you already know it. Now it's their turn. So as you design the instruction, make a concerted effort to get the learners involved. Everyone will benefit.

We started out in this volume implying that designing instruction was a lot of work and did little to dispel that notion as the chapters progressed. On the other hand, there are few tasks which offer so much opportunity for having an impact on another person and getting back so much in return. Therefore, we close by saying that the effort is worth it because, as the old saying goes,

You never learn so much as when you teach another.

Appendix A   Sample Objective and Essay Questions

OBJECTIVE

1) Students will be able to describe the advantages of on-line searching.

OBJECTIVE QUESTION

Which of the following is an advantage of on-line searching that is not characteristic of manual searching?

a) Only items library owns are listed.
b) Small chance of missing important sources.
*c) Ability to combine concepts easily.
d) Browsing capability enhanced.

ESSAY QUESTION

List three advantages of on-line searching that are not characteristic of manual searching.

2) Students will be able to identify key concepts in their statement of the topic to be searched.

Which of the following would be a key concept in searching for information about the use of computers in creative writing? (Circle the letters of all that apply.)

a) Writing
b) Creativity

If we wished to search for information concerning the use of computers in creative writing, what key concepts should be used to select descriptors?

* = correct answer

223

c) Word processing
*d) Creative writing
*e) Computers
f) Robotics

3) Students will be able to list possible synonyms for each concept in a search.

If we were searching for information on the causes of alcoholism and drug abuse among adolescents, which synonym in each set that follows a key concept would be most helpful?

alcoholism:
 a) addiction
 b) behavior disorders
 *c) drinking

drug abuse:
 a) mental disorders
 *b) drug addiction
 c) cocaine

adolescents:
 *a) teenagers
 b) children
 c) students

If we wished to search for information about the causes of alcoholism and drug abuse among adolescents, list three possible synonyms that could be used for each of the following key concepts:

alcoholism

drug abuse

adolescents

4) Students will be able to use boolean operators to group concepts and form a search statement.

Which of the following statements uses appropriate boolean operators to get information about diet for the elderly?

a) diet or elderly

*b) (diet or nutrition) and (elderly or aged)

c) diet and nutrition and elderly

d) (diet and nutrition) or (elderly and aged)

Use boolean operators to combine the following terms so we will get information about diet for the elderly:

diet

nutrition

elderly

aged

5) Given a brief description of available data bases, students will be able to choose those that are appropriate for the topic and explain their reasoning.

Here is a list of data bases and brief descriptions of each. Which would you choose to find information about methods to improve productivity in the public sector for a paper in an advanced management course, and why?

a) *Magazine Index*

b) *Legal Resource Index*

*c) *ABI/INFORM*

Here is a list of data bases and brief descriptions of each. Which would you choose to find information about methods to improve productivity in the public sector for a paper in an advanced management course, and why?

d) *Wall Street Journal Index*
1) Because this data base covers the *Wall Street Journal*
*2) Because this data base contains information on business topics
3) Because this data base covers a broad range of subjects
4) Because this data base has the broadest selection of sources

6) Students will be able to use thesauri to choose appropriate terms and modify their search statements.

Use the ERIC thesaurus to select the appropriately worded search statements for the following topic: the effect of cultural bias on college admissions test scores.

*a) test bias and college entrance examinations
b) cultural bias and admissions test scores and higher education
c) cultural bias and college entrance examinations
d) test bias and admissions tests and higher education

You have been given a thesaurus for ERIC. Use it to create a search statement for the following topic: the effect of cultural bias on college admissions test scores.

Appendix B
Sample Worksheet for Freshman English Library Unit

research paper worksheet

The purpose of this worksheet is to lead you through the steps of a library **search strategy** that you will be able to apply to almost any research project you encounter in other courses. By following a search strategy that leads from background reading, to books located with the aid of the Subject Headings List, to articles listed in both general and specialized periodical indexes, you can make the best use of the time you spend in the library.

Both the nature of college assignments and the complexity of a library system having millions of books require the use of research techniques more sophisticated than those already mastered by most entering students. For this reason the Undergraduate Library (UGL) staff has prepared a series of UGL Study Guides on finding and using different information sources. You will be using four of these Study Guides to complete this worksheet:

★ USING THE LIBRARY FOR RESEARCH

★ FINDING BACKGROUND INFORMATION

★ FINDING BOOKS

★ FINDING ARTICLES IN PERIODICALS

Some of the points covered in the Study Guides may be a review of what you already know, but each one also introduces skills and sources that will be new to you. If you read the Study Guides carefully, follow the search strategy suggested, and allow plenty of time to do your library work, you should be able to find the materials most useful for your topic. The librarians at the UGL Information/Reference Desk welcome your questions. If you are concerned that you may have overlooked some important sources, feel free to ask the librarians for suggestions.

STRUCTURE

The techniques associated with writing research papers are covered in your text and will be discussed in class. Outside class, you will record on this worksheet the steps you take to find material on your topic. In addition, you will make bibliography cards for the books and articles you want to read. The bibliography cards should contain all the information you need for your paper's final bibliography: author, title, publication details, and date. You will also prepare note cards summarizing the relevant material you have found.

-2-

Your instructor will be checking this worksheet before you write your paper so that you will have time to follow through on suggestions. Unless your instructor indicates otherwise, your bibliography and note cards don't have to be handed in until you submit your paper.

Record below the due dates your instructor assigns.

★ Due date for worksheet sections I & II_____

   Your worksheet will be evaluated to see whether you

   1. found an appropriate source for background information on your preliminary topic;

   2. have a workable topic or thesis statement that is not too broad or too narrow for the length of paper assigned.

★ Due date for worksheet section III_____

   By this time you should have

   1. used the Subject Headings List to find the most useful subject headings for your topic;

   2. identified in the Subject Catalog five to ten books that may be relevant.

★ Due date for worksheet section IV_____

   By this time you should have

   1. consulted at least two different periodical indexes (one general and one specialized index);

   2. identified five to ten articles that may be useful.

★ Due date for paper, worksheet, bibliography cards, and note cards_____

   Your paper will be evaluated to see whether you

   1. applied the rhetorical and composition skills covered in this course;

   2. used the format for footnotes and final bibliography that is prescribed by your English handbook;

   3. listed in your final bibliography six to ten references, including an encyclopedia or other background source, books, and periodical articles.

-3-

Section I: STARTING YOUR RESEARCH

Begin by reading the UGL Study Guide USING THE LIBRARY FOR RESEARCH. It gives an
overview of the search strategy you will be following, guidelines for choosing and
narrowing a topic, and instructions for filling out bibliography and note cards.
Record your preliminary topic in the space provided below.

At this stage, you will probably have only a general idea of your topic. After you
complete the next section, you should be prepared to focus on a particular aspect
that interests you.

WRITE DOWN YOUR PRELIMINARY TOPIC:

Section II: FINDING BACKGROUND INFORMATION

Your objectives are to get an overview of your topic and narrow it by following
the steps listed below.

1. Read the UGL Study Guide FINDING BACKGROUND INFORMATION, then choose a source
appropriate for your topic from one of these starting points:

      Social Sciences (page 2 of the Study Guide)

      Humanities (page 3 of the Study Guide)

      Science and Technology (page 4 of the Study Guide)

Use the **index** in the source to find all the pertinent information on your topic.

2. In the space provided below, write down the title of the background source you
have chosen and read the article on your topic. If the source is useful, make a
bibliography card for it and as many note cards as necessary. If there is a
bibliography at the end of the article you have read, you may want to look at some of
the items listed there to find more information. Make a bibliography card for each
item you want to find. If this background source was useful, go on to step 4 on the
next page of this worksheet.

If the background source you used was not useful, list the title in the space
provided below, and go on to step 3. List every background source you try so you
will have a record of the sources you have eliminated.

-4-

3. If your first choice was not useful or if you need more help narrowing your topic, choose another source from the UGL Study Guide FINDING BACKGROUND INFORMATION. In addition to the specialized encyclopedias, consider the general background sources (listed on page 5 of the Study Guide). In the space provided below, write down the title of the background source, read the article on your topic, and make bibliography and note cards as necessary. If this choice is also unproductive, ask for help at the Information/Reference Desk; finding background information on some topics is more difficult than for others.

4. From what you have read so far, decide how you can narrow your topic. The UGL Study Guide USING THE LIBRARY FOR RESEARCH explains how to use background reading to narrow your topic and formulate a thesis statement. Thinking in terms of a question your paper could answer, summarize the main point of your paper in a **thesis** or **topic statement**. Although you may find it necessary to revise this statement later, it will help you focus your research and note-taking. If you have difficulty formulating a thesis or topic statement, talk to your instructor.

WRITE DOWN YOUR THESIS OR TOPIC STATEMENT:

-5-

Section III: FINDING BOOKS

☛ Your objective is to locate books on your topic available in this library by following these steps:

1. Think again about your thesis statement. Then based on the background reading you have already done on your topic, list below any terms you think might be useful for finding books in the Subject Catalog.

LIST KEY TERMS FROM YOUR THESIS STATEMENT:

2. Read the UGL Study Guide FINDING BOOKS. Although books on almost every subject are listed in the Subject Catalog, the subject headings will often be different from the terms you would use to describe your topic.

Read the instructions on the cover of one of the copies of the <u>Subject Headings List</u> (the large red books on the tables near the Subject Catalog).

Look in the <u>Subject Headings List</u> for the terms you listed above to find subject headings relevant to your topic.

List these subject headings in the space provided below. (People and organizations are listed neither in the <u>Subject Headings List</u> nor in the Subject Catalog. Find them in the Name/Title Catalog.)

LIST THE SUBJECT HEADINGS (from the <u>Subject Headings List</u>) USED FOR YOUR TOPIC:

3. Next look in the Subject Catalog for the subject headings you found in the <u>Subject Headings List</u>. As you look at the catalog cards for the books listed under each of these subject headings, fill out bibliography cards for the books that seem appropriate for your topic. **(You should fill out cards for more books than you think you will really need because some of the books you find may not prove useful.)**

-6-

4. Use the LOCATION CHART (attached to the glass wall across from the Information/ Reference Desk) to determine on which floor the books are located. Add the floor numbers to your bibliography cards. Check out some of the books **now** and begin your reading and note-taking. The UGL Study Guide USING THE LIBRARY FOR RESEARCH includes suggestions to help you keep your notes in a clear, usable form.

As you read, look for ideas that support your **thesis statement**. You will supplement and update this information with periodical articles, which you will find by following the steps outlined in the next section of this worksheet.

-7-

Section IV: FINDING ARTICLES IN PERIODICALS

Your objective is to locate periodical articles on your topic by following these
steps:

1. Read the UGL Study Guide FINDING ARTICLES IN PERIODICALS. From the list on
pages 2-4 of the Study Guide, choose one **general index** and one **specialized index** that
seems relevant to your topic.

Look through at least **two years** of each index you select to find articles on your
topic. The subject headings used are usually similar to those in the Subject
Catalog. In the space provided below, write down the titles of the indexes and the
years you look through.

LIST THE INDEXES YOU USED: LIST THE YEARS YOU LOOKED AT:

2. For each article that seems relevant to your topic, fill out a bibliography
card: write down the author's name, the title of the article, the **full title** of the
periodical, the date of the issue, and the page numbers of the article. To identify
these elements of the index entry, pick up a copy of the green handout HOW TO USE
PERIODICAL INDEXES (available on the Index Tables).

If you find fewer than five relevant articles, either look through more years of the
indexes, try a different index, or discuss your problem with a librarian at the
Information/Reference Desk.

3. Turn to the other side of the handout HOW TO USE PERIODICAL INDEXES. This side
is titled HOW TO FIND PERIODICALS. It explains how to use the SERIALS LIST to find
out if the periodicals you need are in UGL or one of the other campus libraries. Add
the library locations to your bibliography cards.

-8-

LAST STEPS

You snould now have

1. a record of the search strategy you used in finding information on your topic;

2. a **working bibliography** made up of the bibliography cards you filled out for background sources, books, and articles;

3. note cards on the material you have already read.

If you need help while you are completing your research, talk with a librarian at the Information/Reference Desk. To get help organizing your notes and writing your paper, check with one of the campus resources described on page 8 of the UGL Study Guide USING THE LIBRARY FOR RESEARCH.

1985-W1
Undergraduate Library
© The General Libraries
The University of Texas at Austin

Appendix C
Sample Journal Guidelines and Entries for an Introductory Sociology Course

GUIDELINES FOR JOURNAL ENTRIES

You have been asked to keep a journal or record of the process you follow in finding information for your library paper. This assignment was made for three reasons. First, by keeping a complete record of the sources you consult, you will know which sources to include in your bibliography and which you have eliminated. Second, after reviewing your search strategy, library reference staff can suggest other resources that might not have occurred to you. Finally, an accurate record of the process you followed and your reasoning behind your choices will assist your instructor in assessing your attainment of the research skills objectives of this course.

Begin by stating your preliminary topic. To ensure completeness and accuracy in your journal entries, please comply with these guidelines.

1. Date each entry.
2. List each source in the order in which you used it, even if it wasn't useful for your topic. A "source" may be a particular book or periodical article or an aid in finding one (e.g., the card catalog, a periodical index, the Serials List, a reference librarian).
3. Under each source listed, describe the following:
   a. why you chose it;
   b. what you expected to find;
   c. what you did find;
   d. how useful you thought the information was for your project;
   e. what your next step was and why you chose it.
4. Follow this procedure until your working bibliography is complete.

JOURNAL ENTRIES

Preliminary topic: Prison Overcrowding

9/27:   I went to the Undergraduate Library and looked for background information in the *Encyclopedia of Crime and Justice* because I expected to find an overview article on my topic. There was a lengthy article on prisons and a section on problems, but it didn't mention overcrowding. Because this encyclopedia was the only specialized encyclopedia on the list that seemed to cover the concept, I looked at the section on general background sources. I then chose *Editorial Research Reports* because its description mentioned a lot of similar topics. It did have a report called "Prison Overcrowding," by Roger Thompson, in the November 25, 1983, issue. I will read the article to help me narrow my topic.

9/29: The article in *Editorial Research Reports* was very helpful. It gave me a good overview of the reasons for the problem and some suggested solutions. I've decided to focus on overcrowding in Texas prisons because the article mentioned Texas as one of the states that was under court order in 1983 to improve prison conditions and because Texas is my home state.

I decided to look for books on my topic because I knew they would give me a lot of information in one place that I could then update with articles. I checked the *LC Subject Headings* and found the heading "Prisons–Texas." When I looked in the subject catalog, however, I couldn't find any books listed under that heading. I guess the library just didn't buy any.

I decided to look at periodical indexes instead because I was sure there must be a lot written about my topic. I chose two specialized indexes from the list, *PAIS* and *Social Sciences Index*, because they include sociology topics. I looked in the last five volumes of each, but I found only three articles on my topic. There were articles on overcrowding in other states, but not much on Texas. I had to leave for class, but I decided to come back and talk to one of the reference librarians.

9/30: I showed my notes to the librarian and she suggested that the topic was too narrow. She said not much has been written on prisons in any one state, so I'd better change my approach to the topic. I looked at the background information again and decided to research "solutions to the prison overcrowding problem." I went back to the *LC Subject Headings*. . .

Appendix D
Sample Checklist for Use of an OCLC Terminal

	Yes	No
1. Selects correct elements of bibliographic entry to search	——	——
2. Selects correct search index for information given (author/title, author, or title)	——	——
3. Enters elements correctly	——	——
4. Chooses correct entry on index screen or group display	——	——
5. Chooses "DLC" record when multiple records are listed	——	——

	Yes	No
6. Identifies field that indicates library's holdings and correctly interprets entry	___	___
7. Identifies LC call number	___	___
8. Uses keyboard appropriately to enter data and move to next or previous screens	___	___

Appendix E   Sample Rating Scale for Freshman English Research Papers

Composition Skills	Outstanding		Average		Poor
1. Topic sufficiently narrowed for length of paper assigned	5	4	3	2	1
2. Thesis clearly stated	5	4	3	2	1
3. Convincing evidence in support of thesis	5	4	3	2	1
4. Synthesis of information found	5	4	3	2	1
5. Interest level of presentation	5	4	3	2	1
6. Organization	5	4	3	2	1
7. Development	5	4	3	2	1
8. Sentence structure	5	4	3	2	1
9. Mechanics	5	4	3	2	1
10. Use of paraphrase and quotation	5	4	3	2	1

	Outstanding		Average		Poor
Research Skills					
1. Adequate number of sources	5	4	3	2	1
2. Variety of sources	5	4	3	2	1
3. Use of scholarly journals	5	4	3	2	1
4. Currency or timeliness of sources	5	4	3	2	1
5. Authority of sources	5	4	3	2	1
6. Footnote form	5	4	3	2	1
7. Bibliographic form	5	4	3	2	1

GRADE ——

Index

For Product Safety Concerns and Information please contact our EU
representative GPSR@taylorandfrancis.com
Taylor & Francis Verlag GmbH, Kaufingerstraße 24, 80331 München, Germany

www.ingramcontent.com/pod-product-compliance
Ingram Content Group UK Ltd.
Pitfield, Milton Keynes, MK11 3LW, UK
UKHW020939180425
457613UK00019B/461